Sewing
in
Circles
Easy Machine
Appliqué
Quilts
Pennie
Horras

Located in Paducah, Kentucky, the American Quilter's Society (AQS) is dedicated to promoting the accomplishments of today's quilters. Through its publications and events, AQS strives to honor today's quiltmakers and their work and to inspire future creativity and innovation in quiltmaking.

Editor: Tracey Johnson
Technical Editor: Helen Squire
Illustrations: Ashley Barnett & Lynda Smith
Graphic Design: Lynda Smith
Cover Design: Michael Buckingham
Photography: Charles R. Lynch

Library of Congress Cataloging-in-Publication Data

Horras, Pennie.
Sewing in circles / by Pennie Horras
p. cm.
ISBN 1-57432-805-0
1. Machine quilting--Patterns. 2. Patchwork--Patterns. 3. Appliqué--Patterns. I. Title

TT835.H59 2003
746.46'041--dc21
2002154919

Additional copies of this book may be ordered from the American Quilter's Society, PO Box 3290, Paducah, KY 42002-3290, or online at www.AQSquilt.com.

DEDICATION

To my Dad, George, who taught me about imagination,
and to Jerry, the love of my life.

CONTENTS

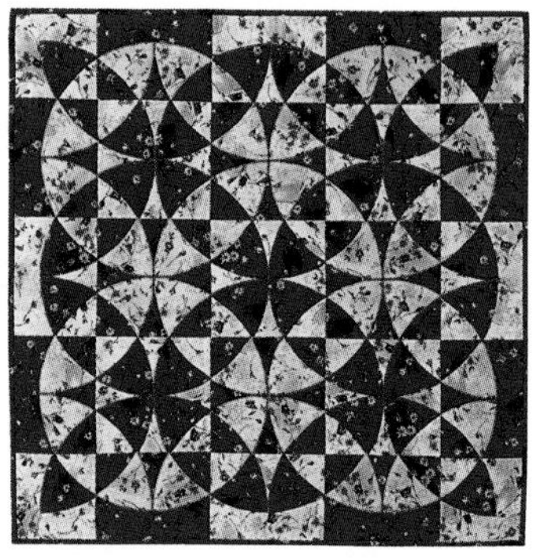

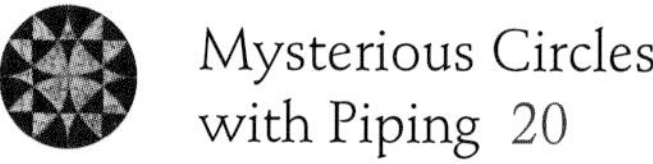

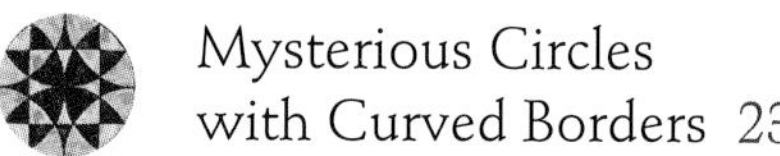

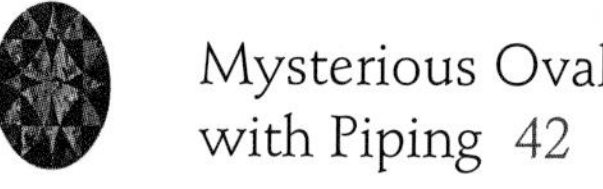

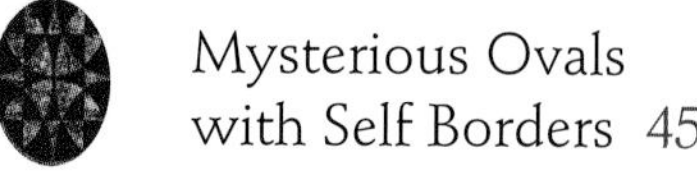

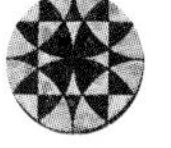

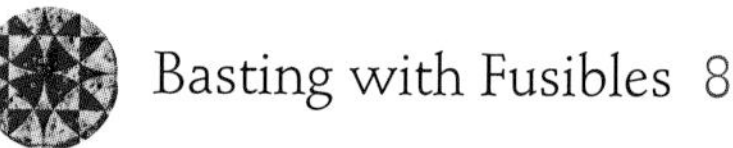

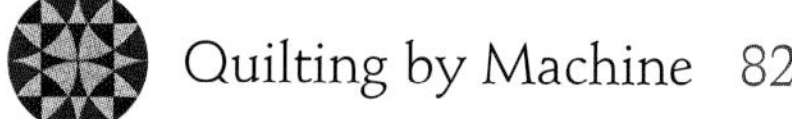

Introduction

When Linda Hiatt, owner of Stitches Galore, Kalona, Iowa, invited me to teach Mysterious Circles classes, I knew it would be the perfect project to test my personal techniques in a hands-on, one-on-one setting. I then realized that quilters and sewers are particularly curious about each other's methods, enjoy a change from the norm, and love to learn and try new techniques.

Sewing in Circles was created for intermediate and experienced quiltmakers. It is designed for sewers who have a friendly, knowledgeable relationship with their sewing machines, are proficient with a rotary cutter, and remember how to cut out paper dolls.

This book is about achieving the results I want, but it is certainly not how it must be done. I hope you will adopt what is useful for your own work and that you will try your hand at making Circle Quilts.

Mysterious Circles

The design materializes into an illusion of interlocking circles. It's intriguing to watch nine blocks, when sewn into a square, make one complete circle. Any number of block rows can be added in either direction.

On my first attempt at making Mysterious Circles, I divided the block into four sections, used the freezer-paper invisible machine appliqué method for the shapes, and sewed the sections together. Not good! Then I discovered fusible appliqué, with four shapes appliquéd to one block. So-so!

Next, a whole shape was appliquéd to one block at a time. Then the blocks were pieced into a quilt top. The problem was that most of the shape tips didn't line up, which resulted in broken circles. Finally, it dawned on me to piece the background blocks, add the shapes, and machine appliqué the whole quilt top at once. I found this method more versatile, easier, and quicker, yet it still created the same effect as the original vintage block.

Kitchen equipment got in on the act when a 16" pizza pan provided the pattern for 8" x 8" blocks. Any size of pattern can be drafted by using circular objects around the house.

Traditional pattern names for Mysterious Circles include Winding Ways, Nashville, Four Leaf Clover, Wheel of Mystery, and Robbing Peter to Pay Paul.

Mysterious Ovals

This design is a first cousin to Mysterious Circles. If the Mysterious Circles pattern could be drafted by using a pizza pan, why not try another shape? This oval pattern was drafted by using a roasting pan lid.

Spinning Circles

This design is based on an antique, hand-pieced quilt I saw at a quilt show. The first challenge was to figure out what size to make the pattern shapes and how to place them accurately on a quilt top. Then I had to decide what techniques would accomplish my goals but would still keep the process simple.

Traditional pattern names for Spinning Circles include Daisy Chain, Joseph's Coat, and Peeled Orange.

Simply Circles

This design was right in front of me all along, in the form of an old green and orange hand-pieced quilt top that was hiding among my things. A number of really interesting quilts can be "simply" made using this versatile design.

Traditional pattern names for Simply Circles include Tea Leaf, Compass, Lover's Knot, Lafayette Orange Peel, Circle Upon Circle, Bay Leaf, Pin Cushion, Whispering Leaves, Save a Piece, Melon Patch, and Flower Petals.

Machine Appliqué

The machine appliqué technique used provides a great way to showcase decorative machine embroidery stitches and create stunning quilts. I've used numerous machine embroidery stitches, from a simple zigzag to fancy decorative ones.

I hope you'll feel free to cut your own pieces of fabric and make something that inspires and pleases you. Strive to make your quilts excellent, exciting, and diverse. I also hope you will be prolific – the more you make, the sooner you'll achieve your goals. Have fun, care about your quilts, follow your own intuitions, and let inspiration and creativity flourish.

Mysterious Ovals variation
by Judie Herzog

Starting the Circle

Vintage designs with curved piecing provided the inspiration for the quilt projects presented here, but these easy, updated versions combine shapes cut from fusible web and decorative machine appliqué stitches to create the same eye-delighting effect of the original pieced designs.

Gather your tools and supplies, read the essentials to the style of your choice, and have fun "sewing in circles"!

Tools & Supplies

- Sewing machine with zigzag or decorative stitches
- Machine needles for piecing, 70/10 or 80/20
- Machine needles for embroidery, 75/11 or 90/14
- Machine needles for quilting, 75/11 or 90/14
- Machine open-toe appliqué presser foot, if available
- Walking foot for machine quilting (optional)
- Rotary cutter with a sharp blade
- Rotary cutting mat
- Sharp scissors
- Rulers for rotary cutting and squaring up
- Steam iron
- A large, flat ironing surface is helpful (see page 13)
- Poster board/lightweight cardboard, up to 13" x 17"
- Freezer paper
- Fine-point permanent markers
- White chalk roller marker
- A variety of fabric markers and pencils
- Small, round sandpaper self-stick grips
- Lightweight fusible interfacing
- Basic sewing tools and supplies

Specialized Supplies

- For Mysterious Circles with curved borders, a 16" diameter circular object, such as a 16" pizza pan
- For Spinning Circles and Simply Circles, a 6" x 24" ruler with a 60° line
- Optional: A compass to design Spinning and Simply Circles quilts in sizes other than those given in the project instructions

Fabrics

Yardage requirements are based on 42"-wide 100% cotton. Fabric suggestions and the amounts needed are given with each project. For a nice finish, pre-wash and dry, spray-size or starch, let dry, and press fabric before cutting.

Threads

- *Piecing thread.* Use a quality cotton.

- *Machine embroidery thread.* Colors should enhance and complement the fabric. If the thread matches one of the fabrics, it will show on the opposite fabric, or it can contrast with all of the fabrics. Black is often an effective choice. Another way to add interest is with variegated thread or by using two or more different thread colors.

- *Bobbin thread.* Use a quality cotton. The bobbin thread can match the decorative thread color. Prewound bobbins are convenient.

- *Machine quilting thread.* Invisible threads come in smoke or clear. The clear works for most fabrics. For the bobbin thread, use a cotton that matches the top fabric color, so if a little bobbin thread comes to the top it won't show. Otherwise, match the thread with the backing.

Fusible Web

Keep several yards of lightweight fusible web on hand. You will be using it throughout the projects in this book.

When purchasing fusible web, check that it is wrinkle-free and well-attached to the paper, especially along the edges. Handle it gingerly because the web can easily release from the paper.

To apply the fusible web, use a steam iron with a clean sole plate. An iron with a non-stick sole plate is helpful when working with fusible web. Trace the design on the paper side of the web and fuse the web to the wrong side of the fabric. I like to turn the fabric over and press again on the right side. Let the fabric cool, then check the fuse by peeling up a corner of the paper. The paper should be smooth and web-free, and the fabric should feel slick.

New fusible webbings appear all the time. Experiment to find which one works best for you. Many different fusing techniques are needed for other fusibles and applications. Read the manufacturer's directions and experiment.

Stabilizers for Embroidery

Freezer paper and lightweight press-and-tear stabilizers are effective when appliquéing with heavier stitches. The stabilizer can be temporarily ironed on the back of the top and torn away after stitching. These types can be a little cumbersome and they are not always compatible with delicate stitches. If using one of these, don't cover the whole back surface. Just cover the small areas where the machine embroidery stitching will be done.

There is a paper stablizer that comes in rolls. Two or more layers of the paper can be applied if a stitch requires a heavier stabilizer. It is easy to tear away after stitching. A light misting of a temporary fabric spray adhesive will help hold it in place. This is a handy product to keep by the sewing machine.

Spray sizing, spray starch from the grocery store, and a spray fabric stabilizer are other choices for stabilizing fabric. To allow for shrinkage, washing and drying the fabric is recommended before using one of these products. Dampen the fabric with the spray, let it air dry completely, and press. Be sure the fabric is sufficiently stiff enough to support the machine embroidery. Experiment with different stabilizers.

Not all stitches need to be stabilized. The blanket and the stretch zigzag stitches are two I use frequently that do not always need to be stabilized. Do not worry about slight tunneling. It should press out. Experiment with a practice block before embroidering the quilt top.

Batting

Fusible fleece is a lightweight, thin batting that is fusible on one side. I like this batting and use it frequently. Cotton, cotton blends, and other low-loft battings work equally well. There are some wonderful new types of battings that are fusible on both sides. I especially like the cotton-polyester blends.

Machine Appliqué for All Quilts

Supplies

- Machine embroidery and bobbin threads
- Machine embroidery needles
- machine open-toe appliqué presser foot
- Fabric stabilizer, if needed
- Practice fabric

Choosing an Embroidery Stitch

Some machines have only the basic stitches. Others have an infinite variety of decorative stitches. Whether distinct or delicate, the stitching adds to the overall effect. Explore and audition various stitches and test different stabilizers on practice fabric. Adjust the top tension to allow a little top thread to show on the back.

Machine Embroidery Stitches

Figures 1–1 through 1–10. Many different machine embroidery stitches are available. Experiment to find the stitch that looks best for each project. Figures 1–1 and 1–2 are the basic zigzag and satin stitches. Notice that some stitches, when sewn, fall entirely on the appliqué shapes, and others are half on and half off the edge of the shapes (Figure 1-3 through 1-10).

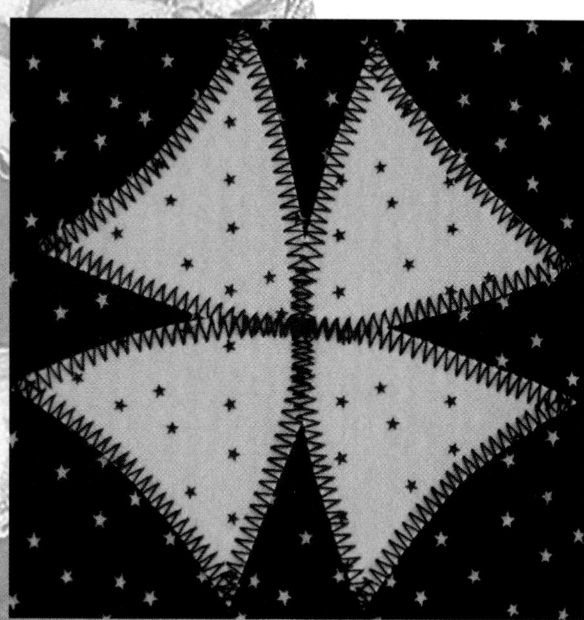

Figure 1–1. Basic zigzag stitch

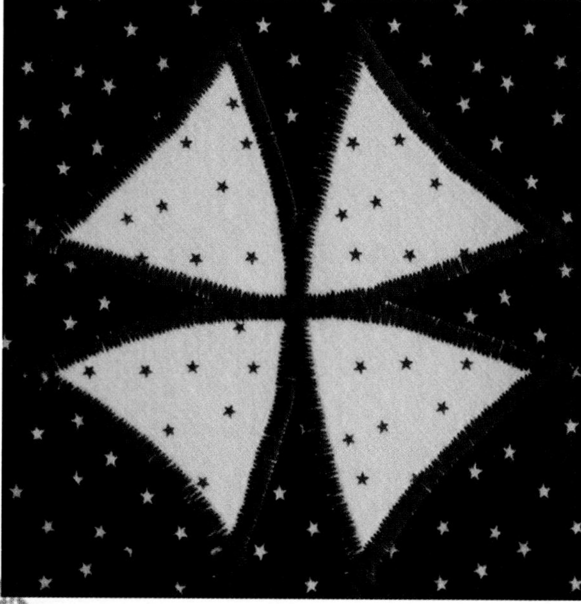

Figure 1–2. Basic satin stitch.

Machine Embroidery Stitches

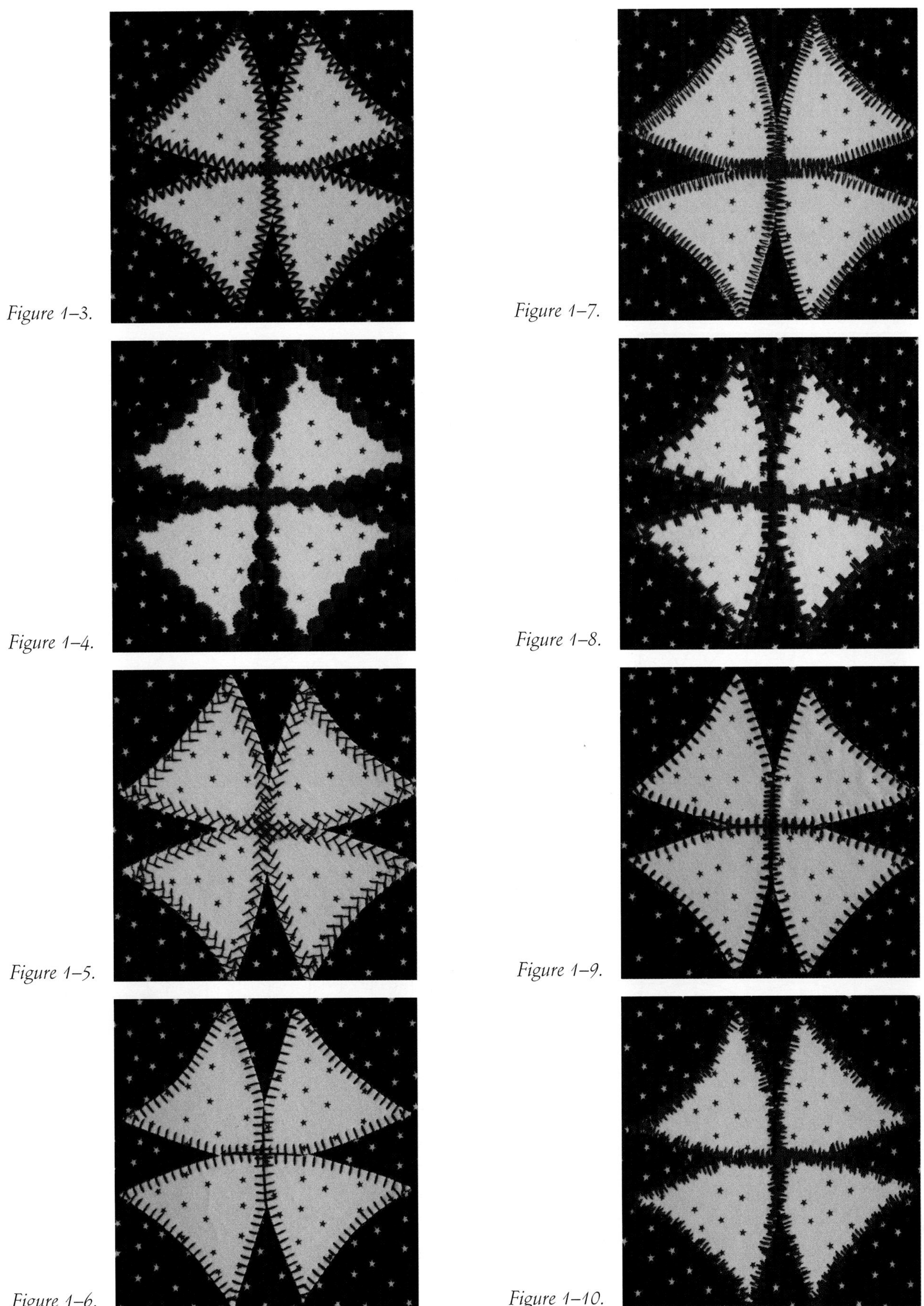

Figure 1–3.

Figure 1–4.

Figure 1–5.

Figure 1–6.

Figure 1–7.

Figure 1–8.

Figure 1–9.

Figure 1–10.

Mysterious Circles & Ovals

If a directional stitch is selected for Mysterious Circles and Mysterious Ovals, keep in mind that a directional stitch must be mirror-imaged when the stitching line crosses from one shape to the next at the background seams. The entire stitch will be on the appliquéd shape. The lines of stitches will look best if sewn side by side at the shape centers (Figure 1–11). Otherwise, for non-directional stitches, follow the Project Essentials for Mysterious Circles and Mysterious Ovals and the stitching sequence diagrams provided with each project.

Spinning Circles, Simply Circles

If using a directional stitch for Spinning Circles and Simply Circles, stitch one side of a row of shapes, pivot, and stitch the other side of the row, with no need to mirror-image the stitching (Figure 1–12). However, if the quilt is too large to pivot, sew one side of the row, go back to the top, mirror image the stitch, and sew the other side of the row. For non-directional stitches, follow the Project Essentials for Spinning Circles and Simply Circles and the stitching sequence diagrams provided with each project.

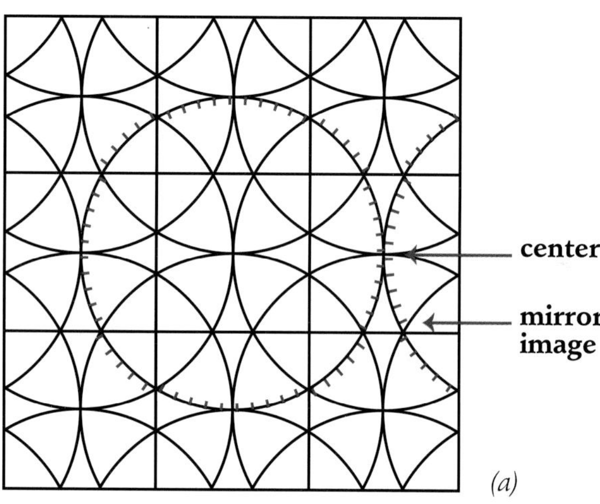

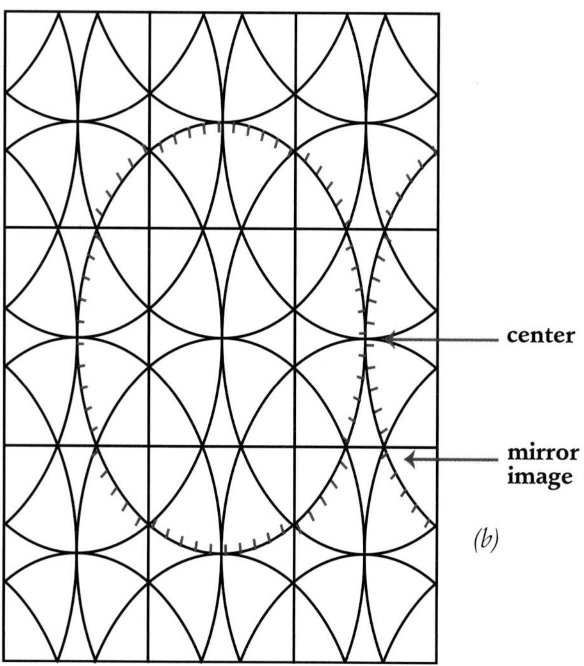

Figure 1–11. (a) Mysterious Circles. (b) Mysterious Ovals. If a directional stitch is selected for these designs, the stitch must be mirror-imaged when the stitching line crosses from one shape to the next.

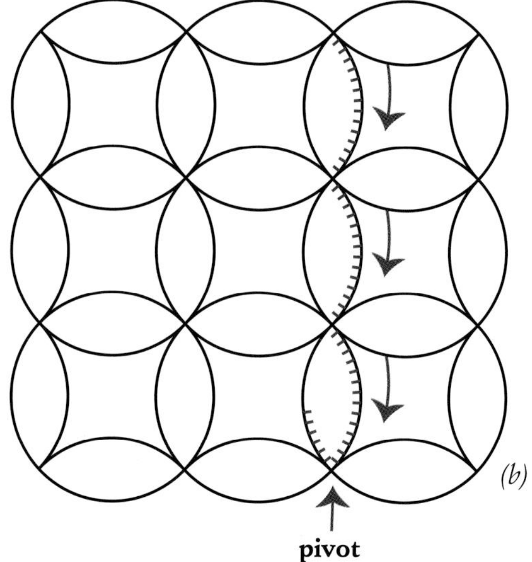

Figure 1–12. (a). Spinning Circles. (b) Simply Circles. If a directional stitch is selected for these designs, the stitch does not have to be mirror-imaged if the quilt is small enough to pivot. Stitch one side of a row of shapes, pivot, and stitch the other side of the row.

Challenge

Advanced quilters may want to do the machine appliqué and quilting all at once. After the shapes are fused and ready for appliqué stitching, layer the quilt and do the machine appliqué through the batting and backing. Try this on practice fabric first. Use a complementary backing fabric and thread colors. The quilt will be reversible, with decorative stitching on both sides. This method is especially suitable for specific styles of quilts with self-borders. I do not recommend it for a first project.

Making an Ironing Mat

Ironing mats are firm and lightweight and can be used as portable design boards. They are easily stored flat and are inexpensive to make. Two large mats lined up side by side make a wonderful work surface for pressing a large quilt top. Ironing mats make great gifts and group projects. Ironing mats are used in all my classes, and they are at the top of my must-have tool list. Mats are especially helpful for the projects in this book.

Supplies for a 24" x 24" Mat

- *Cover.* Trigger cloth, 100% cotton twill or a similar sturdy fabric in a light neutral color, enough for one 30" x 30" cover. This size allows for a 3" wrap to the back of the mat.
- *Padding.* A firm-finish batting, enough for two 24" x 24" layers.
- *Base.* Two 24" x 24" ceiling tiles with flat edges, ½" thick. Choose the least porous tile available. Two ceiling tiles, layered together, assure that heat from the iron does not go through to the bottom side. A piece of 24" x 24" brown paper placed between the tiles adds an extra vapor barrier.
- Staple gun and ⅜" staples
- Duct tape
- Scissors

Mat Assembly

Optional.
Finish the raw edges of the fabric cover.

Lay the 30" x 30" fabric cover on a flat surface. Center the two layers of 24" x 24" padding on the cover. Place one ceiling tile, white side up, on the padding. Place the brown paper on the tile. Layer the second tile, white side down, on the brown paper. Taping the tiles together at the corners with duct tape will help keep them from slipping. Wrap the cover around the edges to the back of the top tile. Wrap and staple the corners first, then staple in several places along each edge. Cover the staples and edges of the cover with long strips of duct tape. This keeps the staples in place and keeps them from scratching surfaces (Figure 1-13).

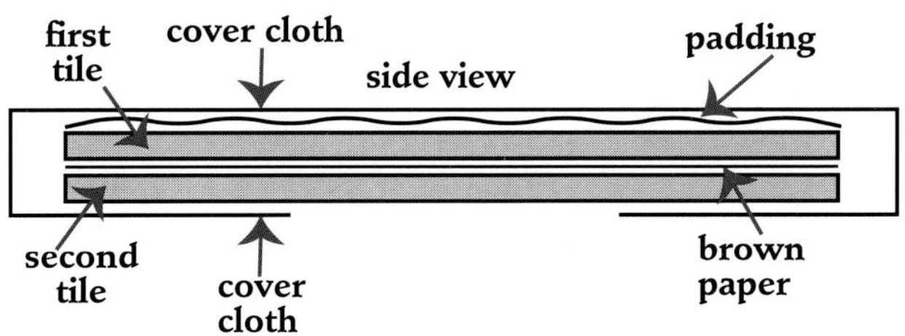

Figure 1–13 (a). Side view of ironing mat.

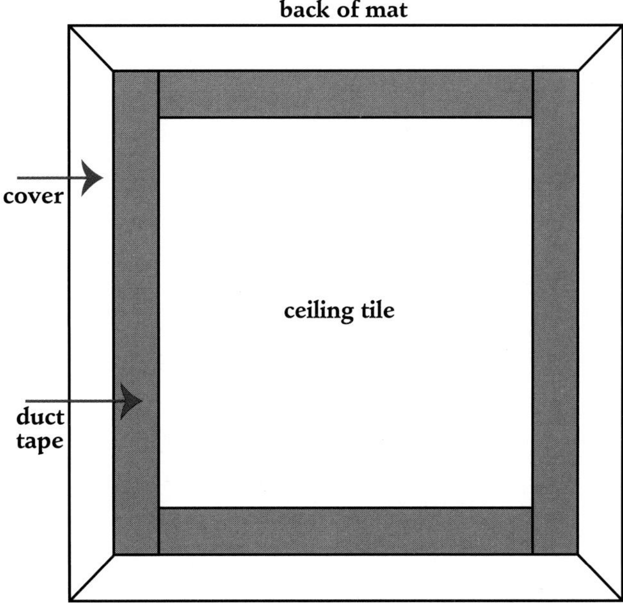

Figure 1–13 (b). Pull cover to the back and tape in place.

Mysterious Circles
by Pennie Horras

MYSTERIOUS CIRCLES & OVALS

PROJECT ESSENTIALS

The tools, techniques, and construction for Mysterious Circles and Mysterious Ovals are basically the same, and the exceptions and fabric requirements are detailed in the projects. Each project will require one or more templates and a placement guide. The terms "self borders" and "seamless borders" mean that the borders are included in the initial piecing, not added later.

Fabric Suggestions

Choose complementary fabrics. They can be any colors, with a subtle or a strong contrast. Using equal quantities of each will create the illusion of interlocked circles or ovals. It's amazing how different the same design can look by simply changing the fabric "flavors." Even the most mundane fabrics come to life in these quilts. Audition fabrics in your favorite color schemes. Even though the quilt projects show specific fabric value arrangements, they can be rearranged to suit personal preference.

Templates & Placement Guides

Supplies

- Freezer paper
- Poster board
- Sharp scissors
- Little round sandpaper self-stick grips

To make a template, trace the pattern on a piece of freezer paper 1" larger all around than the pattern. Iron-fuse the paper to a piece of poster board. The paper will stick long enough to cut along the traced lines. Label each template with the corresponding letter, and affix the little sandpaper grips to the back.

For large templates whose patterns are given in quarters or halves, fold the freezer paper square into quarters. Using the folds as guides, trace the quarter-pattern in one fourth of the freezer paper. Rotate the tracing paper to trace the templates in the next quarter section. Continue rotating the paper and tracing the template until the entire shape has been copied.

Mysterious Circles

For Mysterious Circles designs, use Template A, page 98, and Template B on pages 99. Each project indicates which templates are needed for that project.

Which Fabric Where?

Can't decide at first which fabric to use for the border and binding? Buy the larger amount listed in the project instructions for each fabric. Determine where to use them as the quilt is being assembled.

If you like scrappy quilts or have a collection of fat quarters, the principle for fabric selection is the same: remember the obvious contrast. Fabric arrangements can be planned or random.

Take note of directional and pictorial elements when choosing and cutting fabrics. Build the background first and plan the shapes accordingly. Each shape can be precision cut or a large shape (Template A, page 98) can be cut into two or four pieces and mixed up on the quilt top.

The size of the quilt can be enlarged or reduced by adding or subtracting a row or rows of blocks. The design always works.

To help you place your appliqué pieces on the fabric accurately, you will need to make a cardboard placement guide. To make a placement guide for Mysterious Circles quilts, cut a piece of poster board in an 8" square. With a pencil, mark the square in quarters and mark arrows 1⅛" from each side of the dividing lines on all four sides (Figure 2–1).

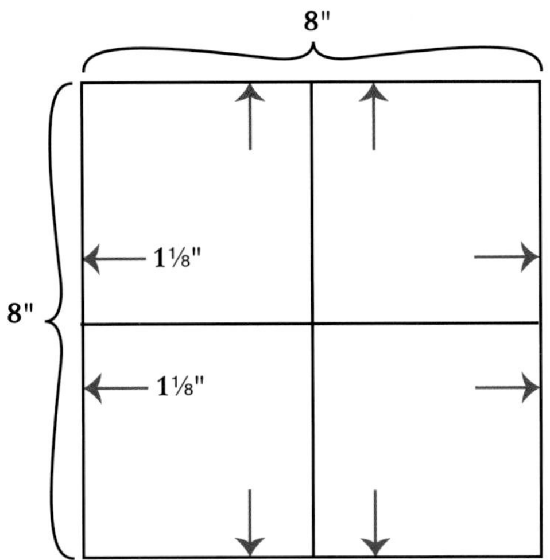

Figure 2–1. An 8" x 8" poster-board placement guide.

Mysterious Ovals

For Mysterious Ovals designs, use Template C. The pattern is on page 100.

To make a placement guide for Mysterious Ovals, cut a piece of poster board in a 5¾" x 7¾" rectangle. With a pencil, mark the rectangle in quarters and mark arrows ⅞" from each side of the dividing lines on the short sides and 1" from each side of the dividing lines on the long sides (Figure 2–2).

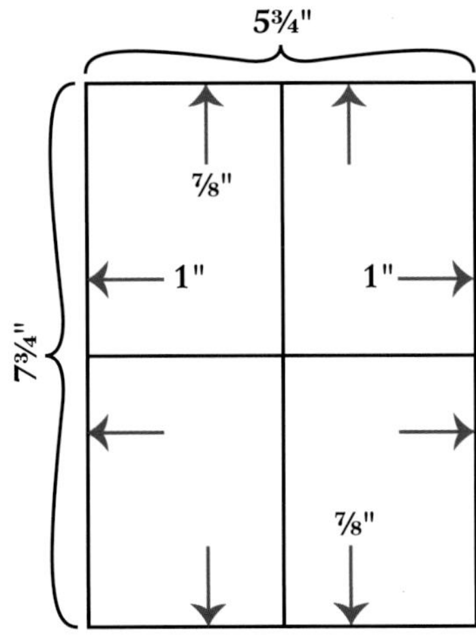

Figure 2–2. A 5¾" x 7¾" poster-board placement guide for Mysterious Ovals designs.

Quilt Top Assembly

Piece the background blocks with a ¼" seam allowance. Piece the blocks in rows, alternating light and dark squares to create a checkerboard. Light and dark color arrangements are illustrated with each project. Press the seam allowances toward the darker fabric. Press again on the other side so the seam allowances lie flat and smooth. Sew the rows together, matching the seams. Where the corner seam allowances converge, press to form a swirl. This will minimize bulk (Figure 2–3).

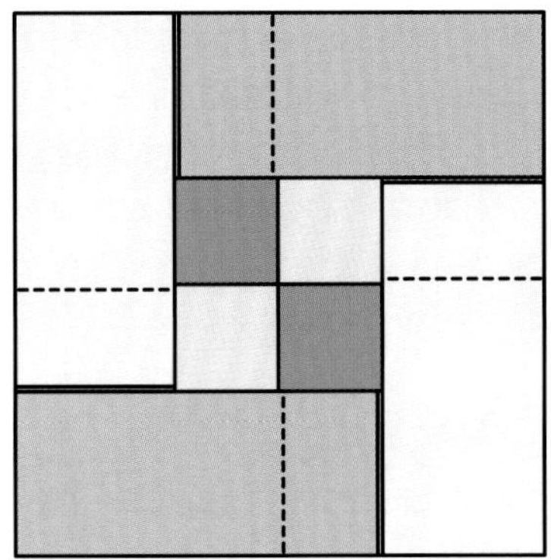

Figure 2–3. Press converging seam allowances in a swirl.

Prepare the shapes by using a fine-tipped permanent marker to trace the template on the paper side of the fusible web. Leave a ¼" space between the tracings. Rough-cut the shapes apart. Arrange the traced paper shapes, fusible side down, on the wrong side of the desired fabrics, leaving space between the tracings. Fuse the shapes to the fabrics and accurately cut out along traced lines (Figure 2–4).

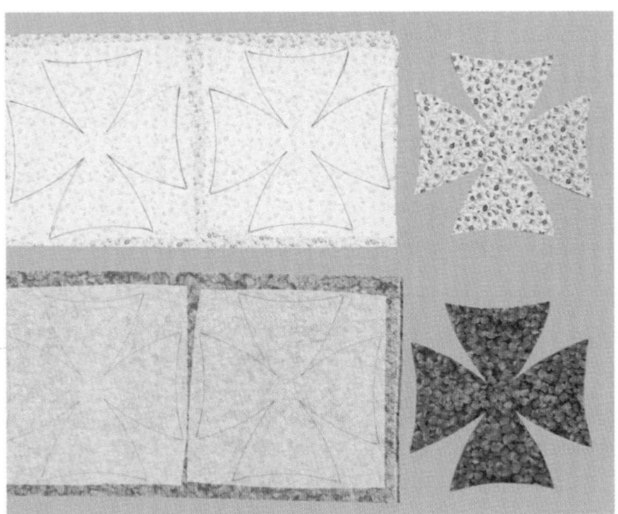

Figure 2–4. Fuse the rough-cut fusible web shapes to the wrong side of the fabric. Cut out on the traced lines.

Which Way is Up?

When using directional print for the appliqué shapes, mark the directional arrow from the template on the fusible web shapes. Align the arrow with the direction of the print when placing web shapes on the fabric.

Set the placement guide on one of the background blocks, and align the guide's edges with the seam lines. Use chalk to transfer all the placement marks to the fabric. The chalk marks will show where to place the tips of the shapes (Figure 2-5). Positioning of the placement guide varies from project to project.

Figure 2–5. Use the placement guide and chalk to mark the background fabric.

Fusing the Shapes

Use the following steps to fuse the shapes to the background blocks.

1. Place and center a dark shape on a light background block. Align the shape tips with the chalk marks (Figure 2-6). The shape tips will meet or slightly overlap the background block seams.

Figure 2–6. Match the shape tips with the chalk marks.

2. Use the tip of the iron to lightly fuse just the shape tips in place. Pat the shape flat with your hand and lightly fuse it in place. If the shape does not lie flat when the tips are fused, slowly lower the iron straight down. The shape will flatten. When fusing, lift the iron straight up and down so as not to wrinkle the edges of the shapes.

3. Continue placing and fusing the rest of the dark shapes.

4. Place and fuse the light shapes to the dark background blocks. The light shape tips will meet or slightly overlap the dark shape tips. It's best if they do, but if some do not quite meet, the decorative stitches will cover the gap.

5. After all of the shapes have been lightly fused, firmly fuse to the quilt top. Press again on the back of the quilt top.

Quilts with Borders

On quilts to which borders will be added after the shapes have been appliquéd, the tips of the shapes should touch or slightly overlap the ¼" outside seam allowance.

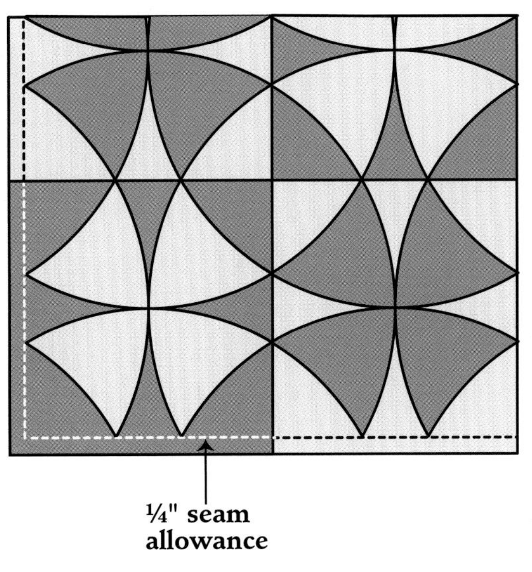

Appliquéing the Quilt Top

1. Make a practice block with the fabrics selected for the quilt. Test different embroidery stitches for the appliqué to find the one that works best and experiment with stabilizers.

2. Apply stabilizer, if necessary, to the back of the pieced top.

3. Appliqué the shapes in sequence, following the diagrams shown with the project.

4. If the project directions say to start sewing a curve just off the raw edge of the quilt top and stop just off the raw edge, it helps to slide a piece of paper partially under the raw edge and start sewing on the paper. Do the same at the end of the curve, sewing off the raw edge and onto the paper.

5. The centers of the Mysterious Circles and Mysterious Ovals shapes will be stitched through four times (Figure 2–7). At the center of each, stitch over previous stitching or next to previous stitching. The stitch selected will determine which. Most stitches will look best if stitched over the previous line of stitches. Notice where the tips meet at the background seams and that the appliqué stitch crosses over from one side of the shape edge to the other. Continue stitching right over the tips and seams. Tips will be covered with stitches.

Figure 2–7. Centers of the shapes are stitched through four times when appliquéd in place.

Finishing the Quilt Top

1. Remove the paper, if it was used at raw edges. Tie off any loose threads, and press the quilt top.

2. Square the top. To keep the corners perfectly square when adding the borders, first fuse a 2" square of lightweight fusible interfacing on the wrong side of the quilt top at each corner. Trim any uneven edges and square up the corners.

3. Add borders. Center and sew the short border strips on two opposite sides of the quilt edges. Press the seam allowances toward the borders and trim the excess border fabric even with the quilt sides. Do the same with the two longer borders.

Finishing the Quilt

Layer the backing, batting, and quilt top. Baste, then quilt. Square up the quilt, then bind and label. See Chapter 4, page 81, Closing the Circle, for finishing ideas.

Projects with Pivots

The sewing sequence diagrams for some projects call for pivots. Use your own technique, or try these suggestions:

For non-directional appliqué stitches, stop stitching at the pivot point with the needle down. Raise the presser foot and rotate the quilt top. Lower the presser foot, raise the needle, and raise the presser foot. Adjust the quilt top slightly in either direction to align the stitches correctly. Lower the presser foot, and continue stitching.

For directional appliqué stitches, stop stitching at the pivot point with the needle down to your left (at its left swing). Raise the presser foot, and rotate the quilt top. Lower the presser foot, and continue stitching.

Mysterious Ovals variation
by Pennie Horras

Mysterious Circles with Piping

by Rhonda Glandorf, 31" x 31

Fabric & Supplies

- ⅞ yard of the darker fabric
- 1⅓ yards of the lighter fabric (includes border and binding)
- Batting 34" x 34"
- 1 yard backing
- 1½ yards of fusible web
- Machine embroidery thread
- Template A for Mysterious Circles
- 8" x 8" placement guide
- Chalk marker

Placement Guide

Mysterious Circles with Piping Project

• Nashville • Wheel of Mystery • Robbing Peter to Pay Paul • Four Leaf Clover • Winding Ways • Robbing Peter to Pay Paul • Four Leaf Clover •

Cutting Blocks, Borders, Binding

Cut strips selvage to selvage.

- **From the lighter fabric:**
  Cut four 8½" x 8½" blocks
  Cut two 4" x 26" borders
  Cut two 4" x 33" borders
  Cut four 2½" strips for binding
- **From the darker fabric:**
  Cut five 8½" x 8½" blocks
  Cut four 1" x 34" strips for piping

Assemble the Quilt Top

1. Piece nine background blocks in a checkerboard pattern with the darker fabric in the center.

2. Prepare the shapes by tracing Template A on the fusible web nine times. Rough-cut apart. Fuse five fusible web shapes to the remaining lighter fabric and four fusible web shapes to the remaining darker fabric. Accurately cut out the shapes.

3. Center the 8" x 8" guide on one of the lighter blocks. With the chalk marker, make a mark on the surrounding darker blocks at each guide arrow. Move the guide and continue marking all of the remaining darker blocks (see Placement Guide above).

4. Begin by centering a dark shape on a light block, matching the shape tips with the chalk marks. Lightly fuse each shape before placing the next one. After all shapes are lightly fused, firmly press the front and back of the quilt top to complete the fusing process.

Mysterious Circles variation
by the author, 32" x 47½"

Appliqué Diagrams

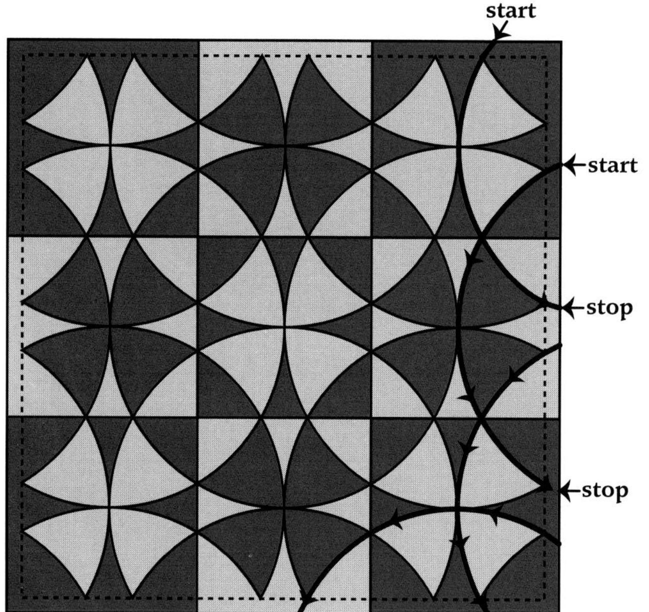

Figure 2–8. Step One.

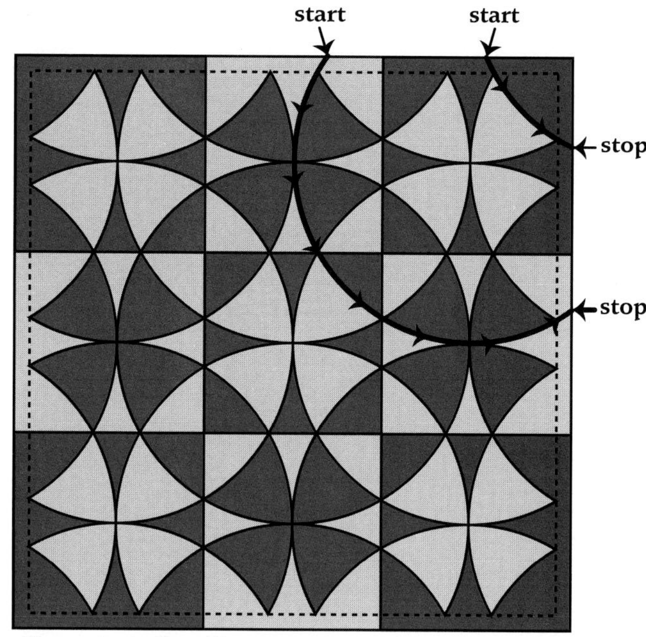

Figure 2–9. Step Two.

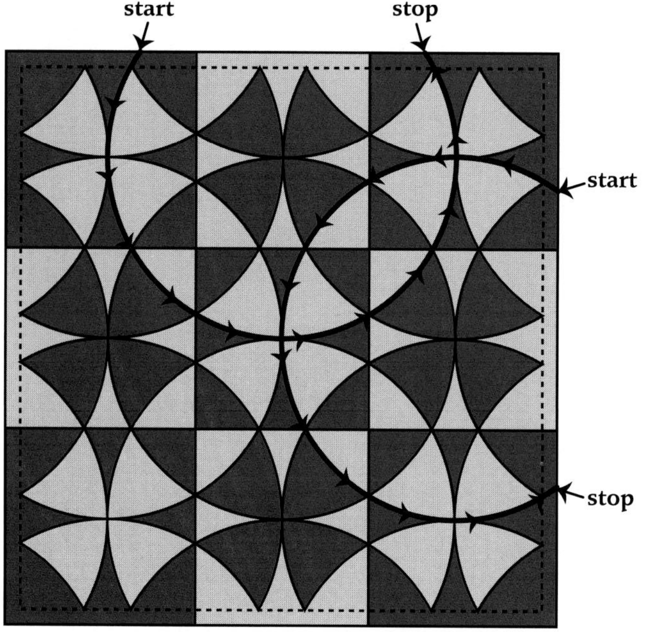

Figure 2–10. Step Three.

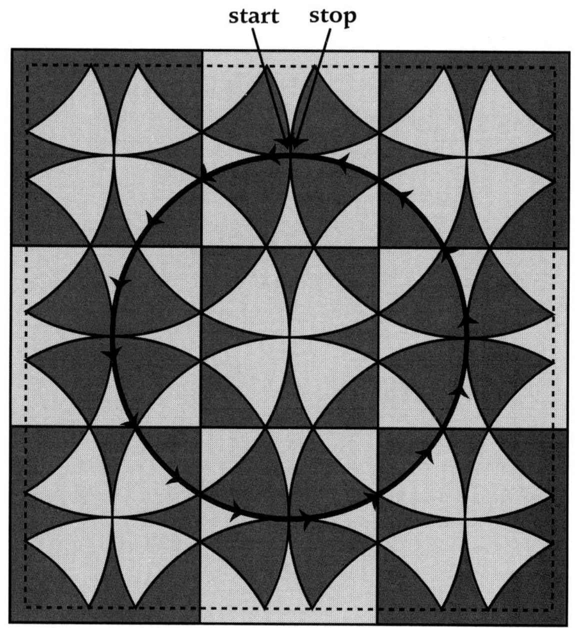

Figure 2–11. Step Four.

Appliqué the Shapes

The diagrams above show the stitching sequence for appliqué. Where appropriate, continue the sequence shown to complete all sides. Refer to the Machine Embroidery Stitches Chart on pages 10-11 for stitching suggestions .

Finish the Quilt

Attach the butted borders. Layer the backing, batting, and quilt top, then quilt around the shapes. Use four 2½"-wide binding strips sewn together, end to end, with diagonal seams to bind the edges. Piping can be inserted before the binding is added to finish the edge, see page 78.

Mysterious Circles with Curved Borders

by the author, 34" x 34"

Fabric & Supplies

- 1⅞ yards of the darker fabric (includes border and binding)
- ⅞ yard of the lighter fabric
- Batting 38" x 38"
- 1⅛ yards backing, 38" x 38"
- 1½ yards fusible web
- Machine embroidery thread
- Template A for Mysterious Circles
- 8" x 8" placement guide
- Chalk marker
- 16" round pizza pan or traceable circular object

Mysterious Circles with Curved Borders Project

• Nashville • Wheel of Mystery • Robbing Peter to Pay Paul • Four Leaf Clover • Winding Ways • Robbing Peter to Pay Paul • Four Leaf Clover •

Placement Guide

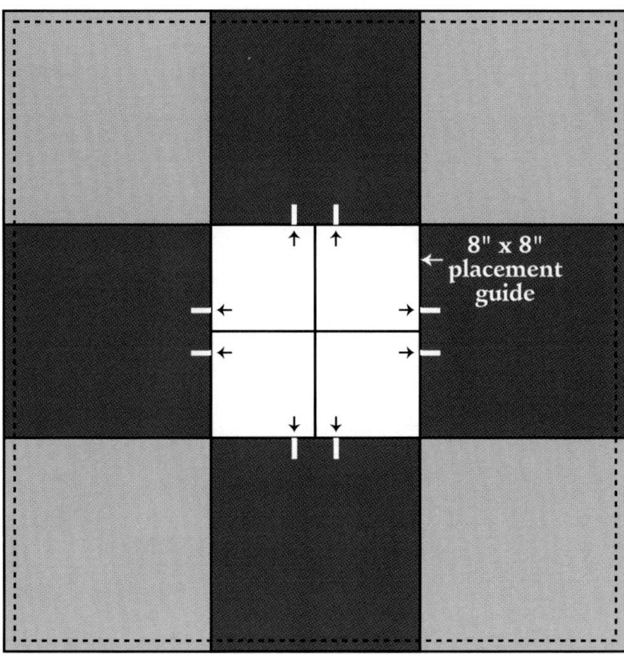

Cut Blocks, Borders, Binding

Cut strips selvage to selvage.

- **From the lighter fabric:**
  Cut five 8½" x 8½" blocks
- **From the darker fabric:**
  Cut four 8½" x 8½" blocks
  Cut two 5½" x 36" borders
  Cut two 5½" x 26" borders
  Cut 2½" bias strips for binding

Assemble the Quilt Top

1. Piece nine background blocks in a checkerboard pattern, with the lighter fabric as the center block.

2. Prepare the shapes by tracing Template A on the fusible web nine times. Rough-cut apart. Fuse five web shapes to the remaining darker fabric and four web shapes to the remaining lighter fabric. Accurately cut out the fused shapes.

3. Center the 8" x 8" guide on one of the lighter blocks. With the chalk marker, make a mark on the surrounding darker blocks at each arrow. Move the guide and continue marking all of the remaining darker blocks (see Placement Guide above).

4. Fuse the shapes to the pieced background. Begin by placing a dark shape centered on a light block, matching the tips with the chalk marks. Lightly fuse each shape before placing the next one. After all the shapes are lightly fused, firmly press the front and back.

Mysterious Circles variation
by the author, 32" x 47½"

Appliqué Diagrams

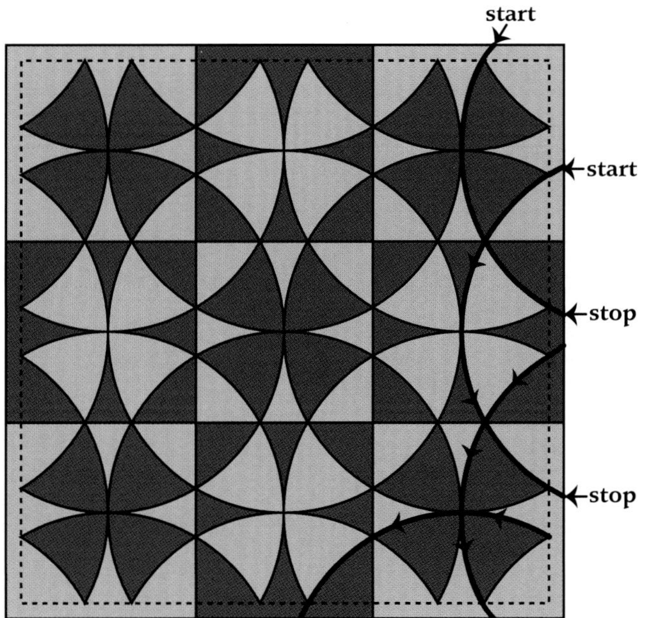

Figure 2–12. Step One.

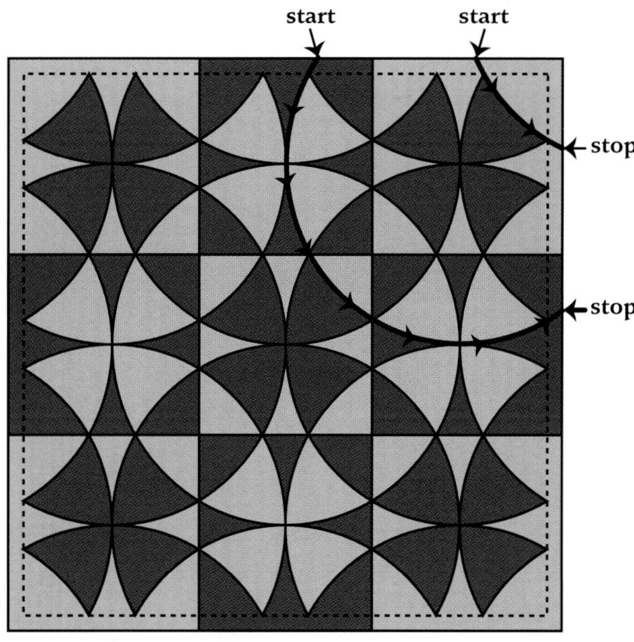

Figure 2–13. Step Two.

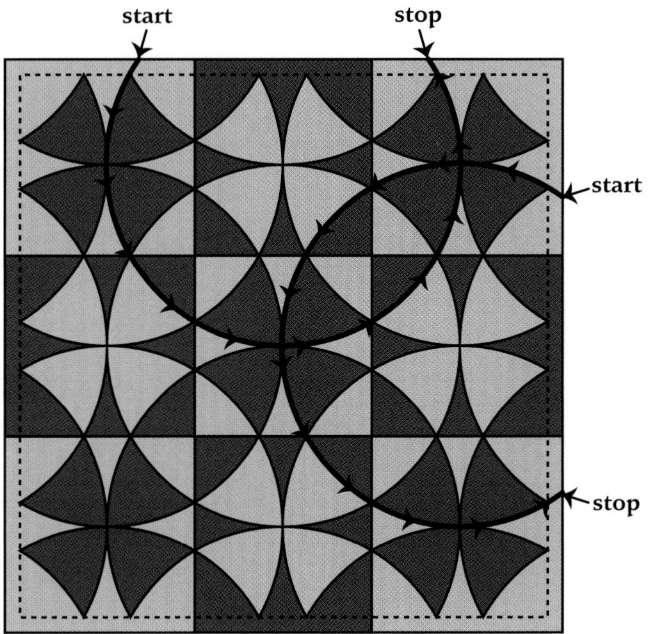

Figure 2–14. Step Three.

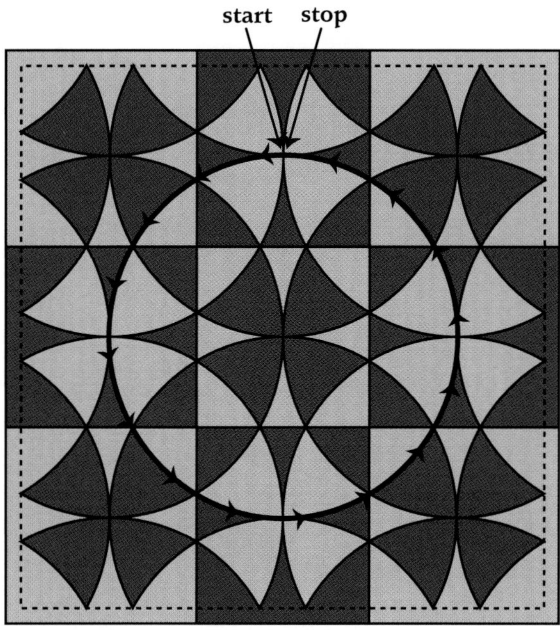

Figure 2–15. Step Four.

Appliqué the Shapes

The diagrams above show the stitching sequence for appliqué. Where appropriate, continue the sequence shown to complete all sides. Refer to the Machine Embroidery Stitches Chart on pages 10–11 for stitching suggestions.

Attach the Borders

Use your favorite techniques to attach the borders, then follow instructions in Edging the Circle, page 75, to create the border curves.

Finish the Quilt

Use your favorite techniques, or see Closing the Circle, page 81, for finishing ideas. Bind the curved edges with bias strips.

Mysterious Circles with Precision-Cut Shapes

By the author, 47" x 47"

Fabric & Supplies

- 1 to 1¼ yards of a directional feature fabric for the precision-cut shapes.
- ⅞ yard of the darker fabric or a combination of darker fabrics that will make twelve 8½" x 8½" blocks.
- 2⅛ yards of the lighter fabric (includes the border)
- ½ yard of a lighter or darker fabric for the binding
- Batting 51" x 51"
- 3 yards backing 51" x 51" (2 panels 26" x 51")
- 3 yards fusible web
- Machine embroidery thread
- Templates A & B for Mysterious Circles
- 8" x 8" placement guide
- Chalk marker

Placement Guide

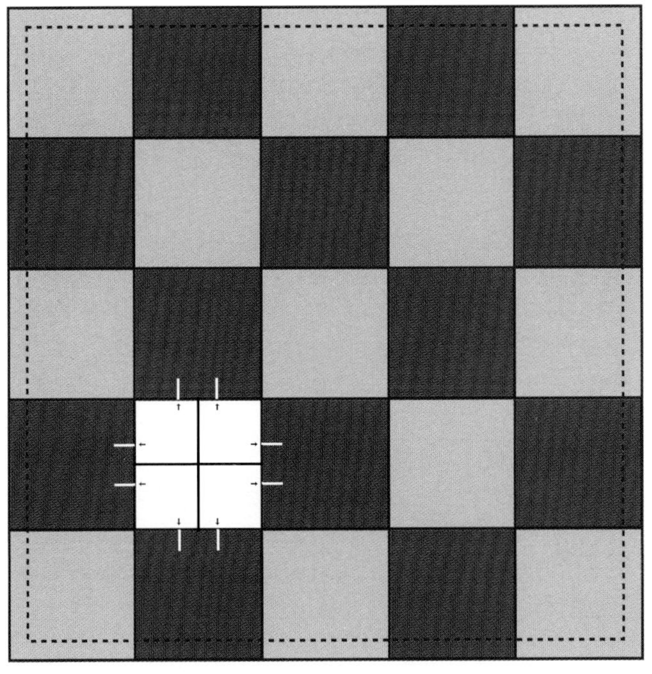

Mysterious Circles with Precision-Cut Shapes Project

• Nashville • Wheel of Mystery • Robbing Peter to Pay Paul • Four Leaf Clover • Winding Ways • Robbing Peter to Pay Paul • Four Leaf Clover •

Cut Blocks, Borders, Binding

- **From the lighter fabric:**
  Cut two 4" x 49" strips for the borders
  Cut two 4" x 42" strips for the borders
  Cut thirteen 8½" x 8½" blocks
- **From the darker fabric:**
  Cut twelve 8½" x 8½" blocks
- **From the lighter or darker fabric:**
  Cut five 2½" strips for binding

Assemble the Quilt Top

1. Piece twenty-five background blocks in a checkerboard pattern, with a block of the lighter fabric as the 8½" x 8½" center square.

2. Prepare the light shapes by tracing Template A on the fusible web twelve times. Rough-cut apart. Fuse the web shapes to the remaining lighter fabric, and cut them out accurately.

For the precision-cut shapes, trace Template B on the fusible web fifty-two times. Rough-cut the shapes apart. Align the center tip of each shape at the same place on the directional fabric design as shown. Fuse to the fabric and accurately cut the shapes (Figure 2–16).

Figure 2–16. Align the center tip of each fusible web shape at the same place on the directional fabric design.

3. Center the 8" x 8" placement guide on one of the lighter blocks . With the chalk marker, make a mark on the surrounding darker blocks at each arrow. Move the guide, and continue marking all of the remaining darker blocks .

4. Before placing the precision-cut shapes on the background blocks, make a little hole in the

exact center of the placement guide with an awl or sharp scissors point (Figure 2-17). The hole needs to be just big enough for the head of a straight pin to slip through.

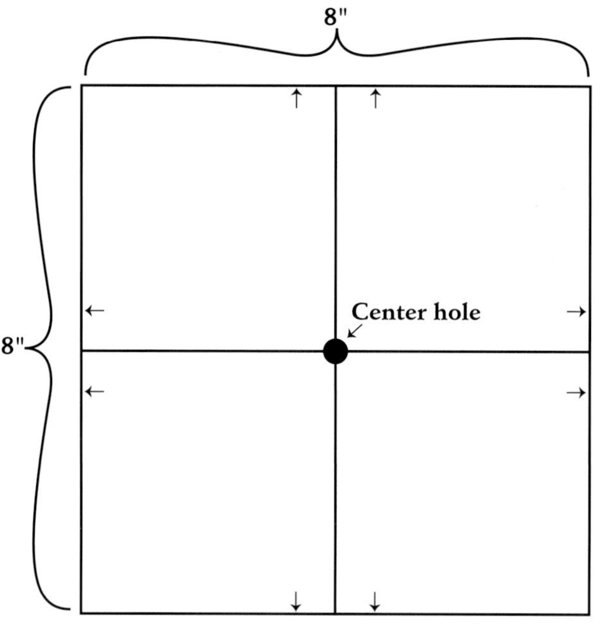

Figure 2-17. Pierce the center of the placement guide.

5. Center the placement guide on a lighter block and stick a straight pin through the hole (Figure 2-18a) straight down into a padded ironing surface underneath. Lift the guide off the pin, without pulling the pin out. To position the precision-cut shapes, place the center tips of four shapes so they just touch the pin, with the outer tips of the shapes aligned with the chalk marks (Figure 2-18b). Lightly fuse the shapes. Continue until all precision-cut shapes are fused in place.

6. Fuse the light shapes to the darker background blocks after all precision-cut shapes have been fused. Firmly press the front and the back after all pieces have been lightly fused.

Appliqué the Shapes

The diagrams on the following two pages show the stitching sequence for appliqué. Continue the sequence shown to complete all sides.

Finish the Quilt

Attach the butted borders. Layer the backing, batting, and quilt top, then quilt around the shapes. Use six 2½"-wide binding strips sewn together, end to end, with diagonal seams to bind the edges. (See Closing the Circle, page 81, for finishing tips.)

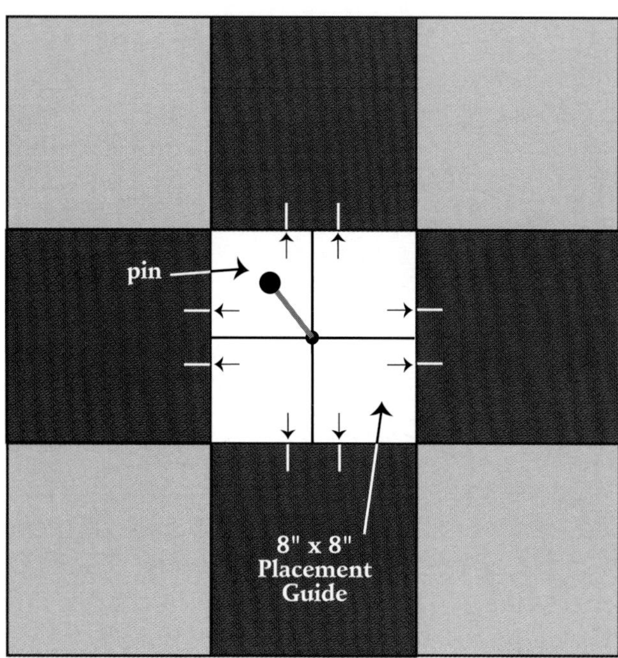

Figure 2-18a. Center the guide on a lighter block, and stick a straight pin through the hole in the center. Leave the pin in place, and lift off the guide.

Figure 2-18b. Position the precision-cut pieces so the center tips touch the pin.

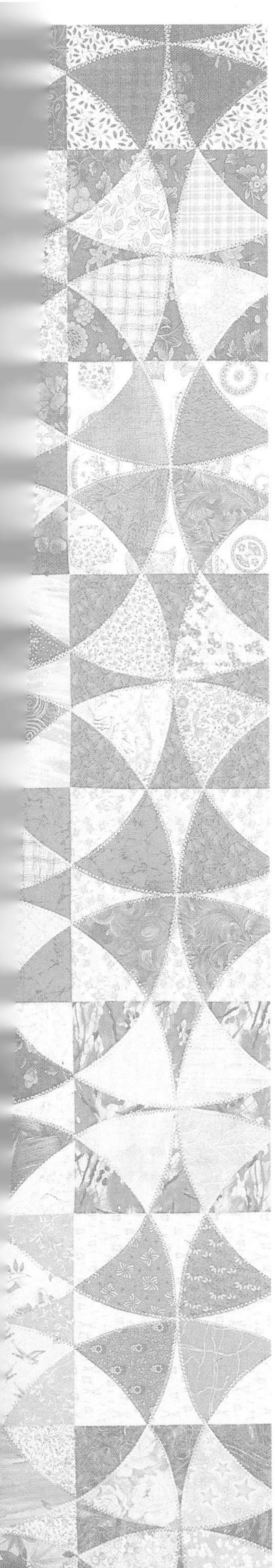

Appliqué Diagrams

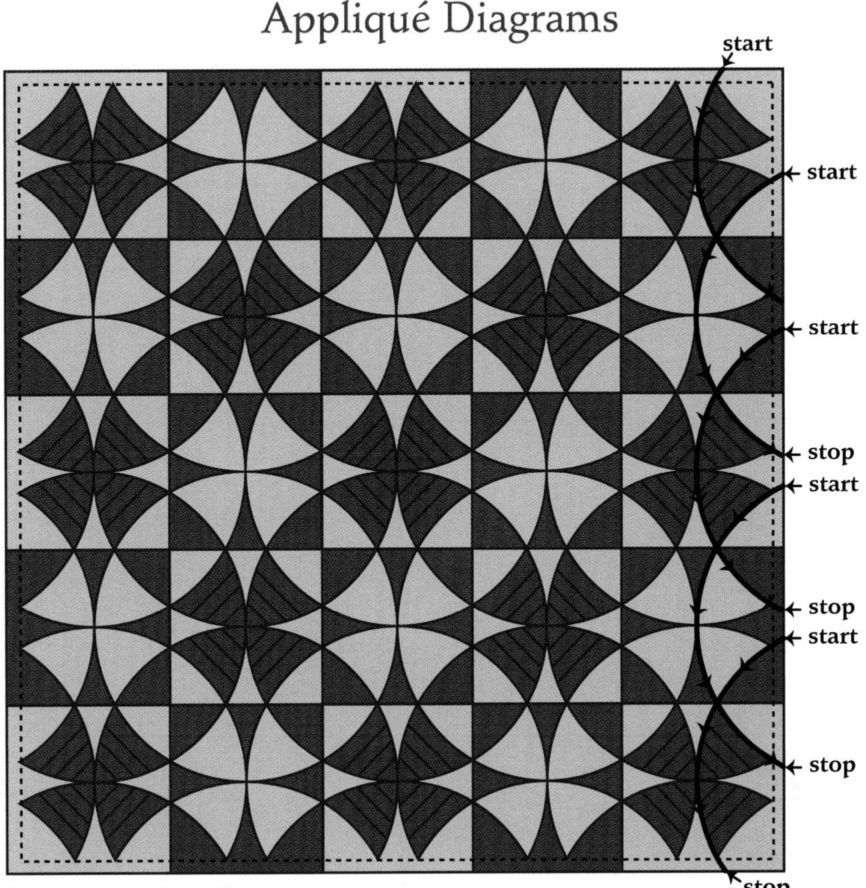

Figure 2–19. Step One.

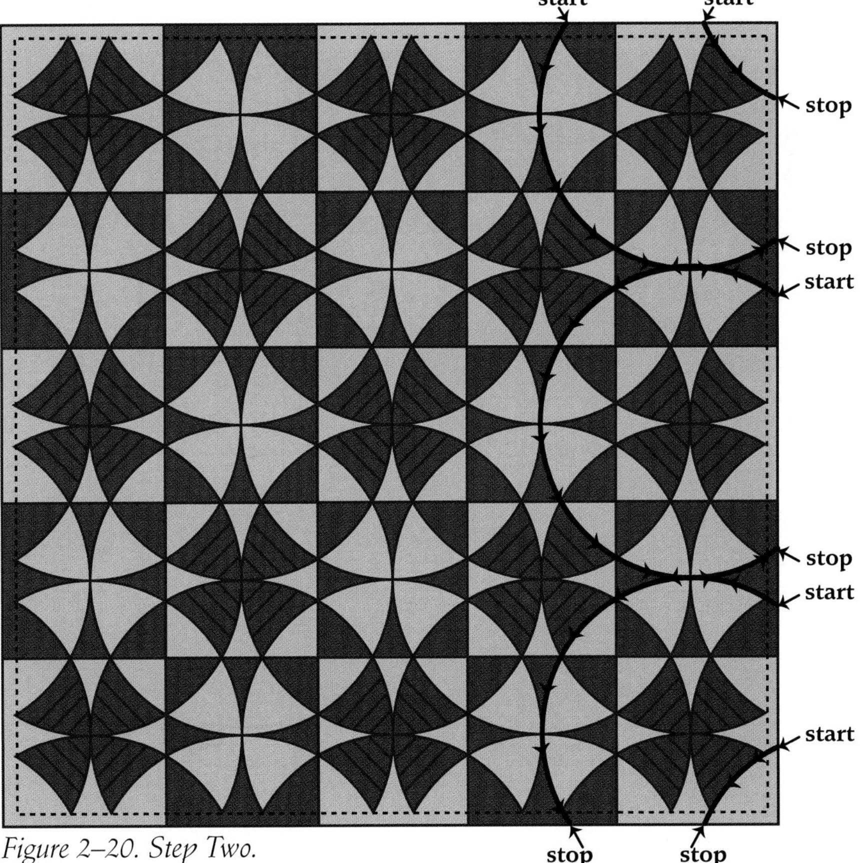

Figure 2–20. Step Two.

Appliqué Diagrams

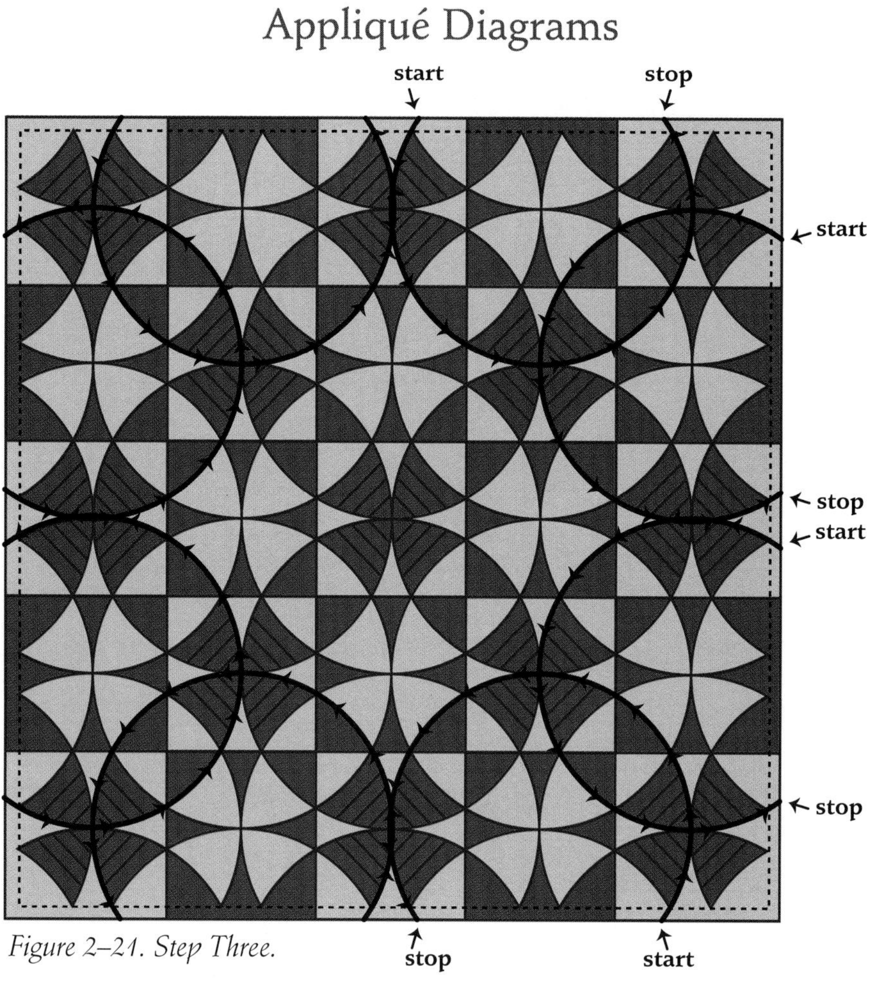

Figure 2–21. Step Three.

Figure 2–22. Step Four.

Mysterious Circles with Self Borders I

By the author, 36" x 36"

Fabric & Supplies

- 1½ yards of the darker fabric (includes fabric for the binding)
- 1¼ yards of the lighter fabric
- Batting 40" x 40"
- 1¼ yards backing 40" x 40"
- 2¼ yards fusible web
- Machine embroidery thread
- Template A for Mysterious Circles
- 8" x 8" placement guide
- Chalk marker

Mysterious Circles with Self Borders I Project

• Nashville • Wheel of Mystery • Robbing Peter to Pay Paul • Four Leaf Clover • Winding Ways • Robbing Peter to Pay Paul • Four Leaf Clover •

Placement Guide

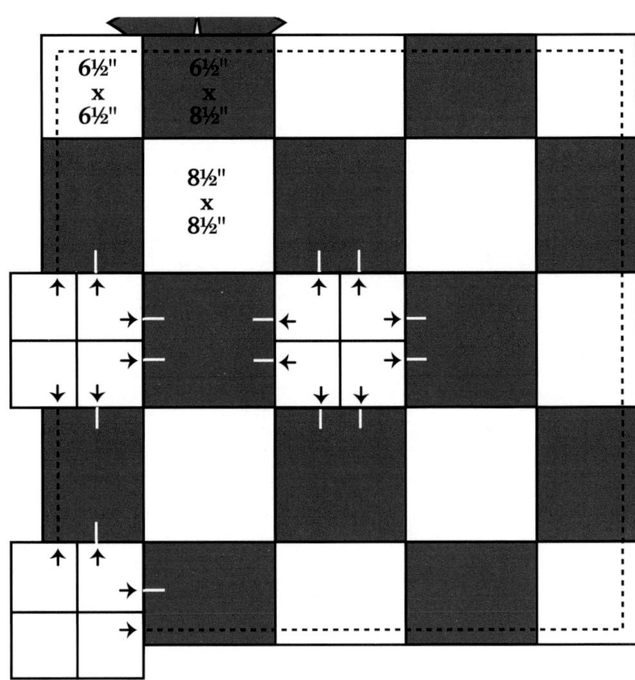

Cut Blocks & Binding

Cut strips selvage to selvage.

- **From the lighter fabric:**
  Cut five 8½" x 8½" blocks
  Cut four 6½" x 8½" blocks
  Cut four 6½" x 6½" blocks
- **From the darker fabric:**
  Cut four 8½" x 8½" blocks
  Cut eight 6½" x 8½" blocks
  Cut four 2½" strips for binding
- Stack the blocks by size and color. There will be 25 blocks.

Assemble the Quilt Top

1. Piece twenty-five background blocks, following the diagram above for placement of different sized blocks. Piece the background in a checkerboard pattern with a block of the lighter fabric as the 8½" x 8½" center square.

2. Prepare the shapes by tracing Template A on the fusible web sixteen times. Rough-cut apart. Fuse eight web shapes to the remaining darker fabric and eight web shapes to the remaining lighter fabric. Accurately cut out the shapes.

3. Cut four lighter fabric shapes in half. Cut two darker fabric shapes in half. Cut one darker fabric shape into quarters (Figure 2–23).

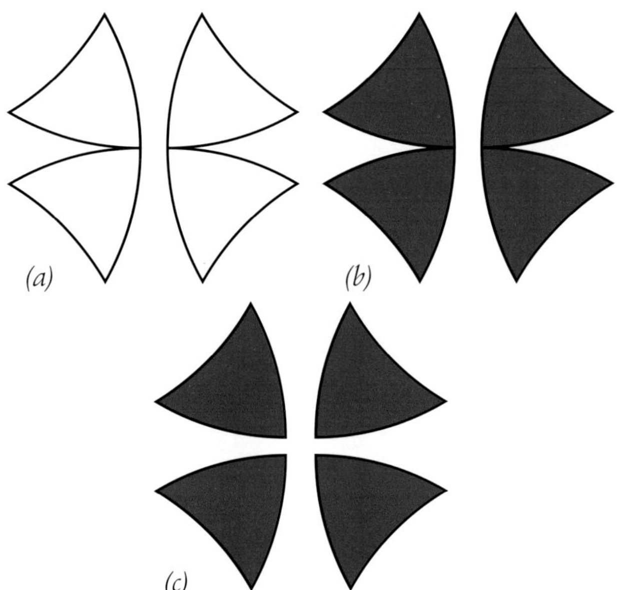

Figure 2–23. (a) Cut four lighter fabric shapes in half; (b) Cut two darker fabric shapes in half; (c) Cut one darker fabric shape into quarters.

4. Center the 8" x 8" guide on one of the lighter blocks. With the chalk marker, make a mark on the surrounding darker blocks at each arrow. Move the guide, and continue marking all of the remaining darker blocks. The guide will extend off of the fabric on the edge and corner blocks.

5. Fuse the shapes to the pieced background by centering a dark shape on a light block and matching the tips with the chalk marks. Refer to the diagram for the placement of partial shapes (Figure 2–24). Lightly fuse each shape before placing the next one. After all shapes have been lightly fused, firmly press the front and back of the quilt top.

Figure 2–24. Fuse whole shapes to the center blocks. Fuse partial shapes to the edge and corner blocks.

Appliqué the Shapes

The three diagrams show the stitching sequence for appliqué. Continue the sequence shown to complete all sides.

Finish the Quilt

Layer the backing, batting, and quilt top, then quilt around the shapes. Use five 2½"-wide binding strips sewn together, end to end, with diagonal seams to bind the edges. See Closing the Circle, page 80, for professional binding tips.

Appliqué Diagrams

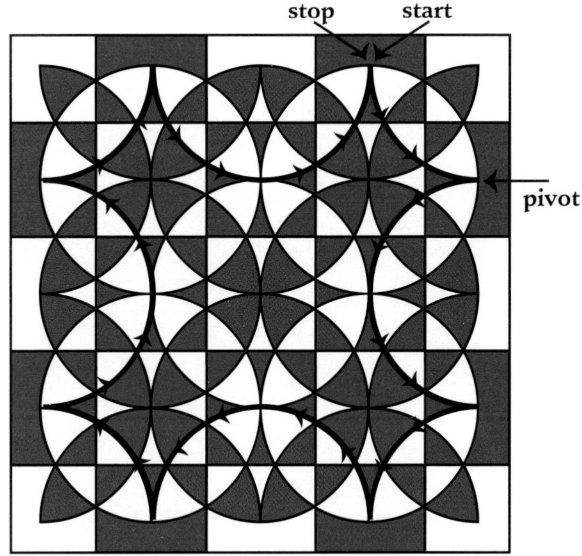

Figure 2–25. Step One.

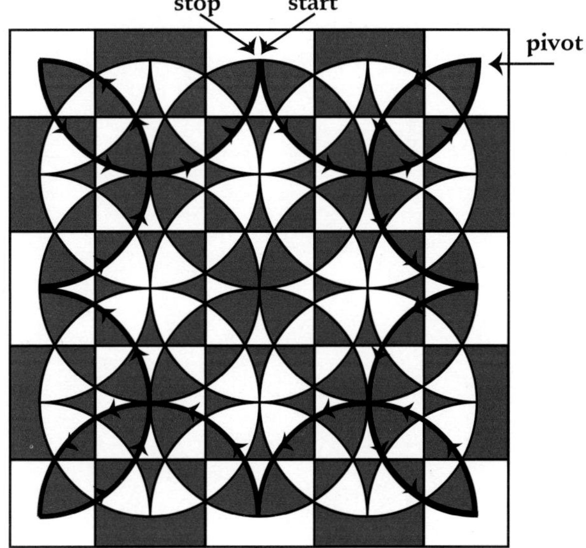

Figure 2–26. Step Two.

Figure 2–27. Step Three.

Mysterious Circles with Seamless Borders

By the author, 42" x 42"

Fabric & Supplies

- 1⅛ yards of the darker fabric
- 1⅛ yards of the lighter fabric
- 1¾ yards of a contrasting fabric for the seamless border and binding
- Batting 46" x 46"
- 2¾ yards backing 46" x 46" (2 panels 24" x 46")
- 2½ yards fusible web
- Machine embroidery thread
- Template A for Mysterious Circles
- 8" x 8" placement guide
- Chalk marker

Placement Guide

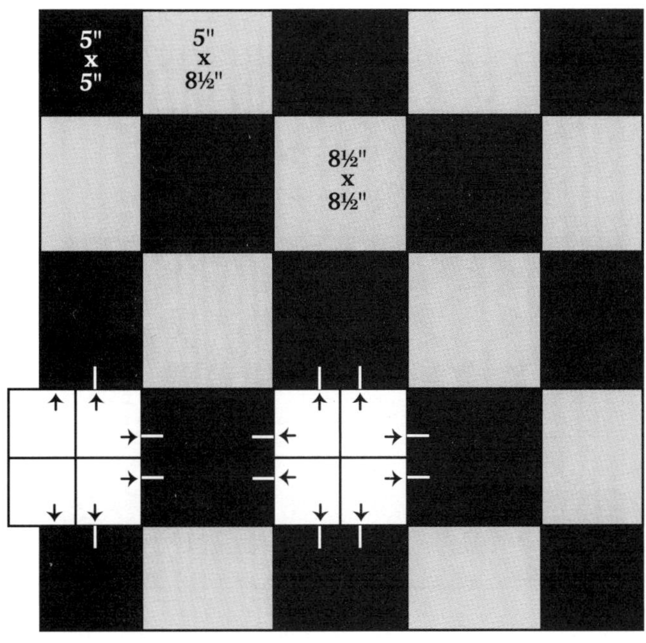

Mysterious Circles with Seamless Borders Project

• Nashville • Wheel of Mystery • Robbing Peter to Pay Paul • Four Leaf Clover • Winding Ways • Robbing Peter to Pay Paul • Four Leaf Clover •

Cut Blocks & Binding

Cut strips selvage to selvage.

- **From the lighter fabric:**
  Cut four 8½" x 8½" blocks
  Cut eight 5" x 8½" blocks
- **From the darker fabric:**
  Cut five 8½" x 8½" blocks
  Cut four 5" x 8½" blocks
  Cut four 5" x 5" blocks
- Stack the blocks by size and color.

Assemble the Quilt Top

1. Piece the background blocks in a checkerboard pattern following the diagram above for placement of color and block sizes.

2. Trace Template A on the fusible web fifteen times. Rough-cut apart. Fuse eight web shapes to the remaining darker fabric and seven web shapes to the remaining lighter fabric. Accurately cut out the shapes.

3. Cut four darker fabric shapes in half and two lighter fabric shapes in half (Figure 2–28).

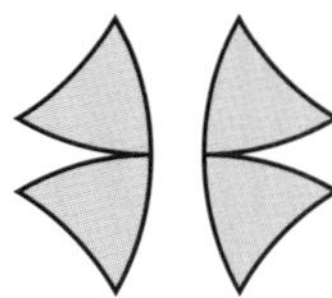

Figure 2–28. Cut four darker fabric shapes and two lighter shapes in half.

4. Center the 8" x 8" placement guide on one of the lighter blocks. With chalk, make a mark on the surrounding darker blocks at each arrow. Move the guide, and continue marking all of the remaining darker blocks

5. Fuse the shapes to the pieced background by centering a dark shape on a light block and matching the tips with the chalk marks. Lightly fuse each shape before placing the next one. There are no shapes on the four corners (Figure 2-29). After all shapes have been lightly fused, firmly press on the front and back.

Figure 2–29. Fuse whole shapes to the center blocks. Fuse partial shapes to the edge blocks. There are no fused shapes in the corner blocks.

Appliqué Diagrams

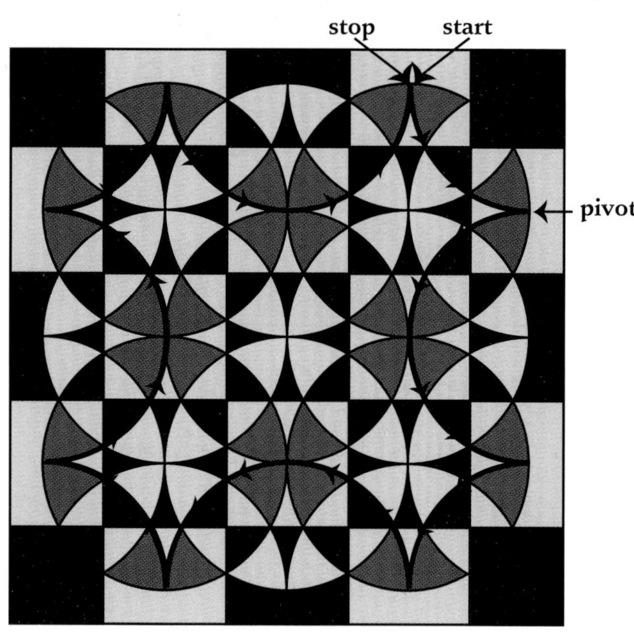

Figure 2–30. Step One.

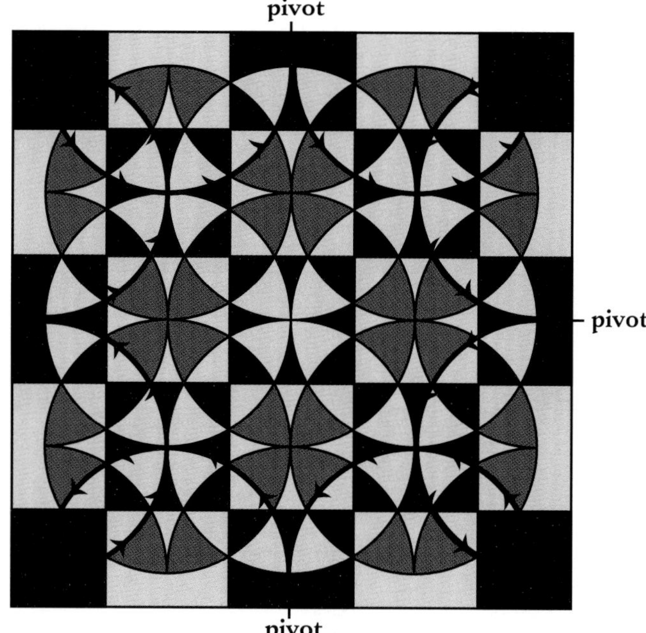

Figure 2–31. Step Two.

Figure 2–32. Step Three.

Appliqué the Shapes

The diagrams above show the stitching sequence for appliqué. Continue the sequence shown to complete all sides. Do not appliqué the outside curves.

Mark Corner Curves

At this point, all of the shapes have been machine appliquéd except the outside curves of the circles. Use the template as a guide to draw the curved lines that will complete the circles at the corners. Follow the curves to cut away the excess fabric (Figure 2–33).

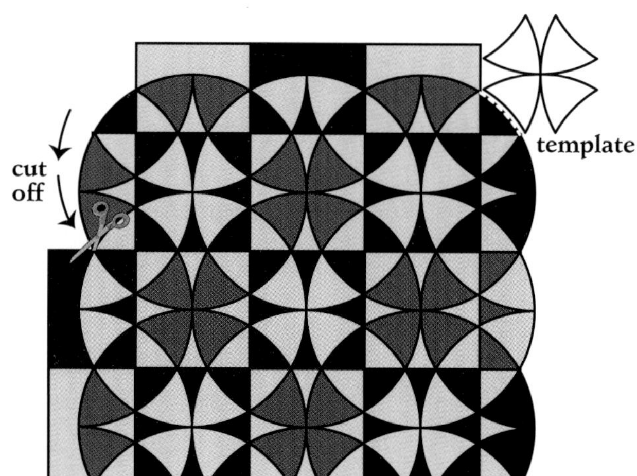

Figure 2–33. Use the template to complete the circles in the corners. Cut excess material away.

Apply Basting Strips

On the wrong side of the quilt top, fuse ½" fusible web basting strips to the outside curved edges. Set the top aside (Figure 2–34). See Closing the Circle, page 80, for basting strips.

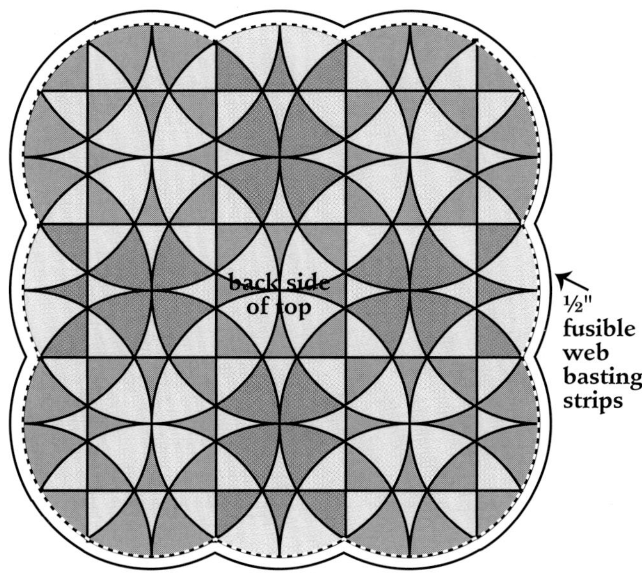

Figure 2–34. Apply basting strips made of fusible web near the edges on the wrong side of the quilt top.

Seamless Borders

1. Measure the width of the border fabric, selvage to selvage. Cut a square this size. It is not necessary to cut off the selvages, because they will help keep the fabric piece squared. Any excess fabric will be cut off later. Fold the fabric, right sides together and edges aligned. Press a crease. Do this in both directions, so the creases divide the square in quarters.

2. Remove the paper backing from the basting strips. Position the quilt top in the center of the border fabric. Line up each side of the quilt top centers with the crease lines on the right side of the border fabric, and fuse the top to the border fabric.

3. Appliqué the quilt top to the border fabric around the curved edges. For added assurance, first use invisible thread and a small zigzag to sew the top around the curved edges to the border fabric (Figure 2–35). Then sew the final appliqué stitch over the invisible zigzag stitch.

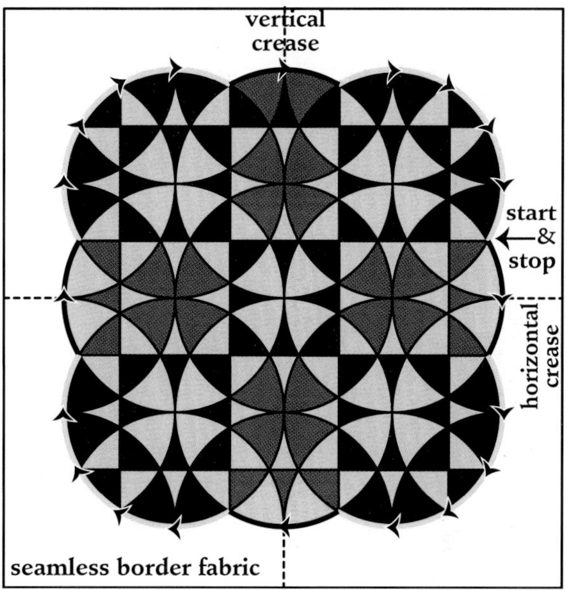

Figure 2–35. The top is centered on the border fabric and appliquéd along the outer curves.

4. Cut away the border fabric from behind the appliquéd circles. Cut along the machine appliqué stitching after the edges have been appliquéd. Cut off the selvages and square up the seamless borders an equal distance from the appliquéd circles.

Finish the Quilt

Layer the backing, batting, and quilt top, then quilt around the shapes. Use five 2½"-wide binding strips sewn together, end to end, with diagonal seams to bind the edges. See Closing the Circle, page 81, for information on squaring up the quilt and making double-fold, straight-grain binding.

Mysterious Circles with Self Borders II

By the author, 60" x 68"

Fabric & Supplies

- The project contains six directional fabrics in three different color families, 1⅜ yards of each: dark & light green, dark & light blue, dark & light red
- ⅔ yard binding fabric: complementary fabric or make candy stripe bias binding from leftover fabrics
- Batting 64" x 72"
- 4¼ yards of backing 64" x 72" (2 panels - 33" x 72")
- 8 yards fusible web
- Machine embroidery thread
- Template A for Mysterious Circles
- 8" x 8" placement guide
- Chalk marker

Placement Guide

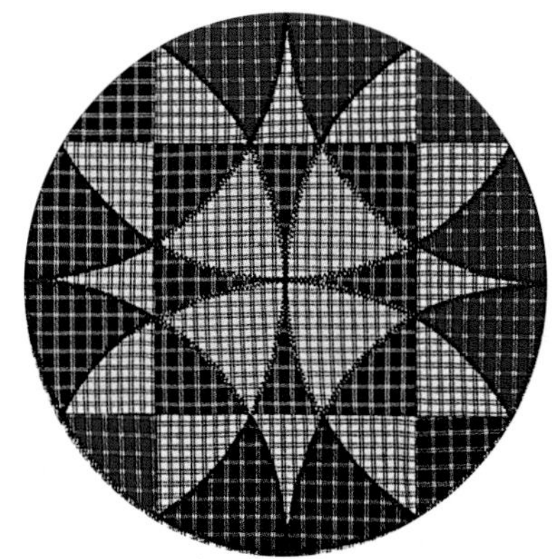

Mysterious Circles with Self Borders II Project

• Nashville • Wheel of Mystery • Robbing Peter to Pay Paul • Four Leaf Clover • Winding Ways • Robbing Peter to Pay Paul • Four Leaf Clover • Winding Ways • Nashville • Wheel of Mystery •

Cut Blocks & Binding

Cut strips selvage to selvage.

- **From the light green fabric:**
  Cut seven 8½" x 8½" blocks
  Cut five 6½" x 8½" blocks
- **From the dark green fabric:**
  Cut seven 8½" x 8½" blocks
  Cut four 6½" x 8½" blocks
- **From the light blue fabric:**
  Cut seven 8½" x 8½" blocks
  Cut four 6½" x 8½" blocks
- **From the dark blue fabric:**
  Cut seven 8½" x 8½" blocks
  Cut five 6½" x 8½" blocks
- **From the light red fabric:**
  Cut seven 8½" x 8½" blocks
  Cut four 6½" x 8½" blocks
  Cut two 6½" x 6½" blocks
- **From the dark red fabric:**
  Cut seven 8½" x 8½" blocks
  Cut four 6½" x 8½" blocks
  Cut two 6½" x 6½" blocks
- Stack the blocks by size and color.
- Cut five 2½" strips to make binding.

Assemble the Quilt Top

1. Piece the seventy-two background blocks, following the placement diagram above and the photo for placement of block sizes and colors.

2. Prepare the shapes by tracing Template A on the fusible web fifty-eight times. Mark the directional lines on the paper shape to line up with the directional fabric, if necessary. Rough cut apart. Position the fusible web shapes on the fabric, following this list of colors. Ten each: dark green, dark red, light blue, light red. Nine each: dark blue, light green.

3. Align the shapes with the fabric's directional lines if necessary. Fuse the web shapes to the fabric. and cut them out (Figure 2–36).

Figure 2–36. Align the fusible web shape with the directional fabric.

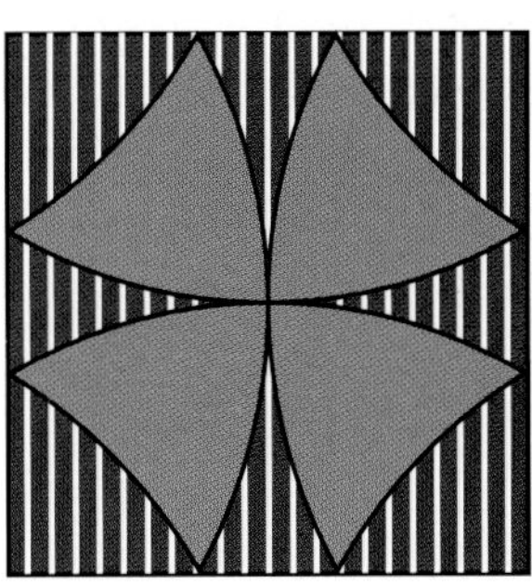

4. Cut the following shapes in half: three dark green, two dark blue, three dark red, two light green, three light blue, and three light red. Cut these shapes into corners: two dark red and two light red. There will be four half shapes left. Use these for practice fabric (Figure 2–37).

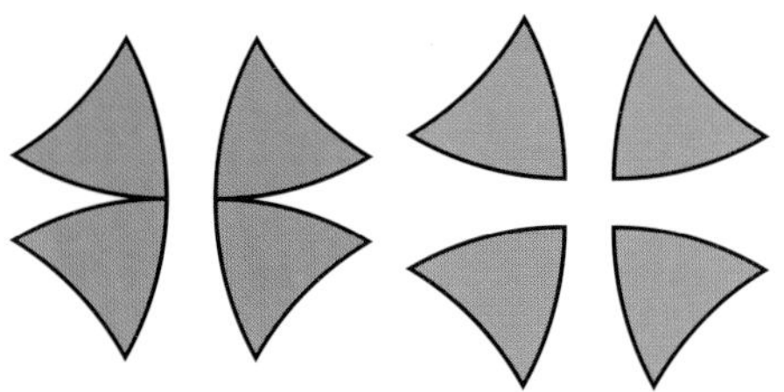

Figure 2–37. Cut shapes in halves and quarters.

5. Center the 8" x 8" guide on any light colored block. With the chalk marker, make a mark on the surrounding darker blocks at each arrow. Move the guide and continue marking all of the remaining darker blocks. The guide will extend off of the fabric on the edge blocks.

6. On larger quilts, mark the background blocks and fuse the shapes as you go along. Begin by centering a dark shape on a light block and matching the tips with the chalk marks. Lightly fuse each shape before placing the next one. Fuse all of the dark shapes first, then the light shapes will automatically line up with the dark ones. After all shapes have been lightly fused, firmly press the front and back.

Appliqué the Shapes

Appliqué the top in sequence following the diagrams. Because there is a considerable amount of machine appliqué, choose a simple, speedy decorative stitch.

Appliqué Diagrams

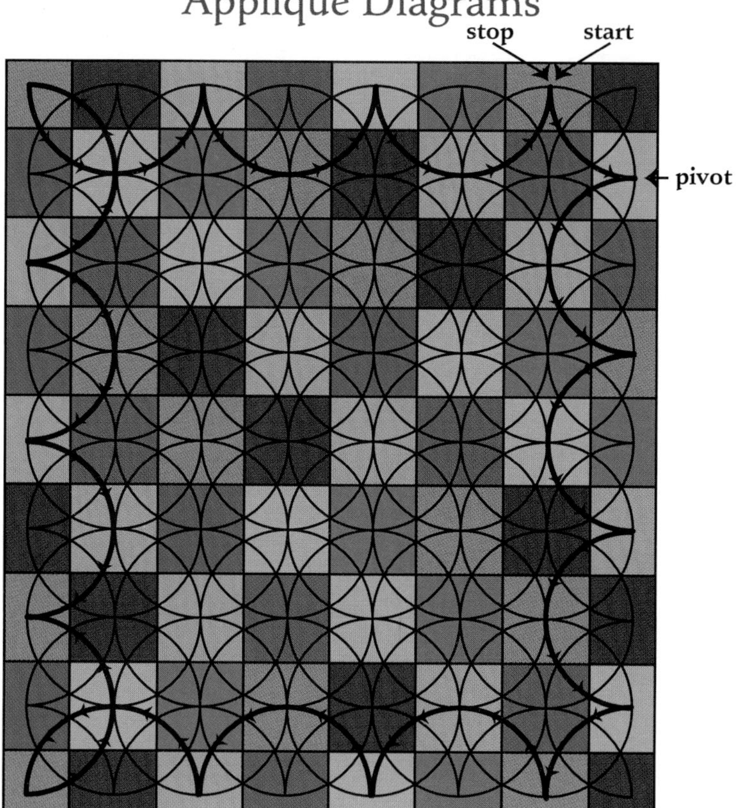

Figure 2–38. Step One.

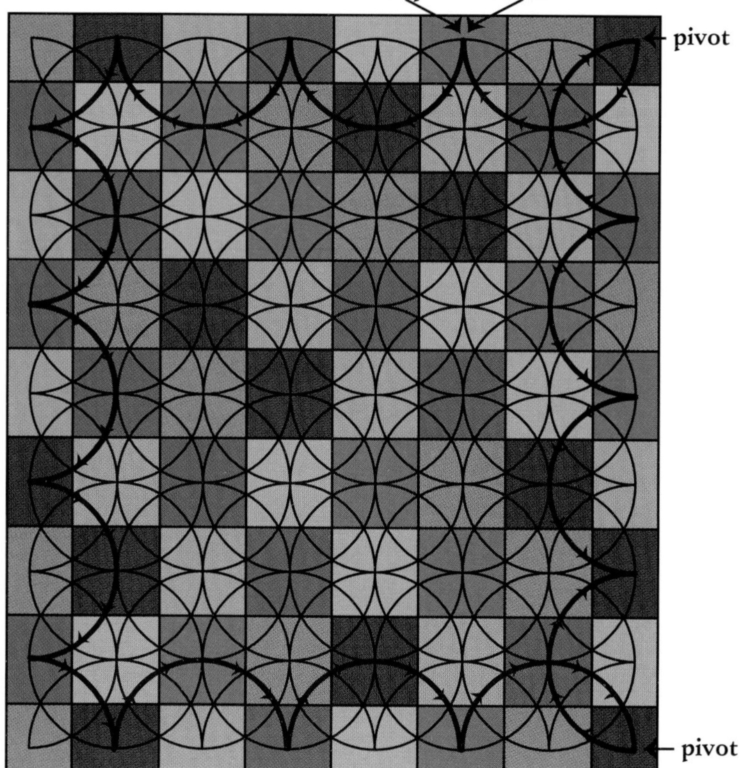

Figure 2–39. Step Two.

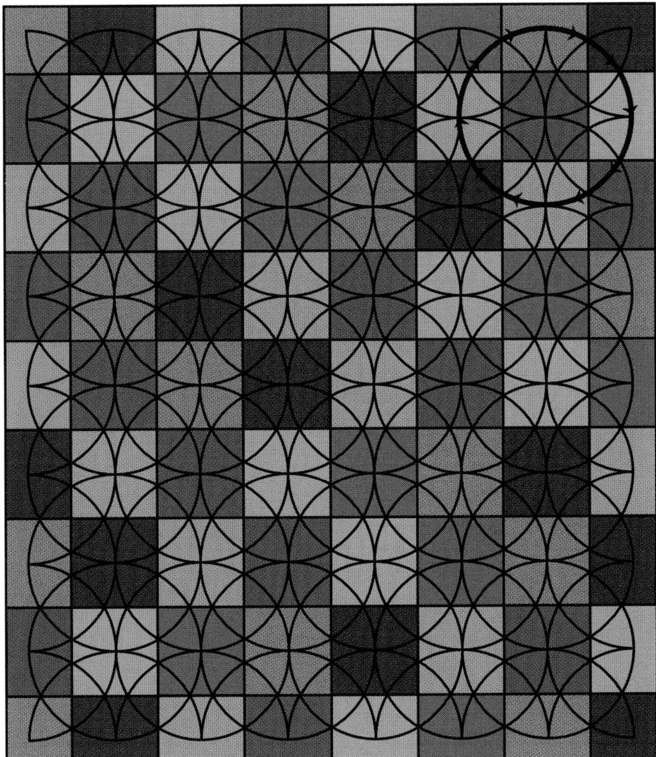

Figure 2–40. Step Three.

Candy-Stripe Binding

1. Use strips to make binding or make candy-stripe bias binding from the leftover fabrics as follows: Cut 1½" strips from long pieces of fabric of equal length. Sew the strips together, alternating the colors until you have a panel about as wide as the length of the strips. Start and end the colors in the same order as they are in the panel. Press the seam allowances open. *In the sample made for this project, the leftover pieces measured 15" long, so a panel 15" x 15" was made.*

2. Cut the panel in half diagonally from corner to corner (Figure 2–41).

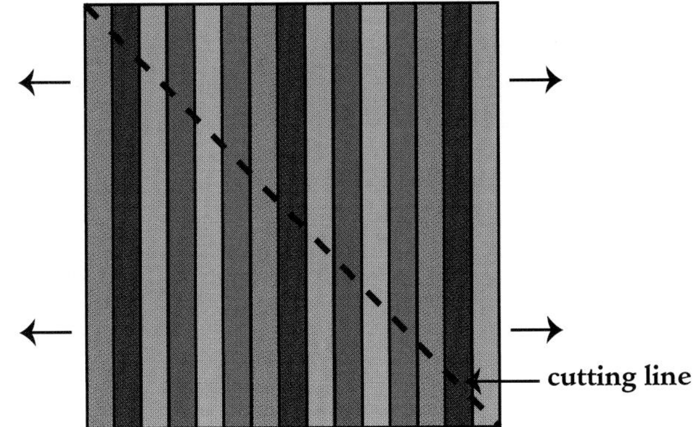

Figure 2–41.

3. Sew the diagonally cut halves back together, matching the arrows as shown in Figure 2–42.

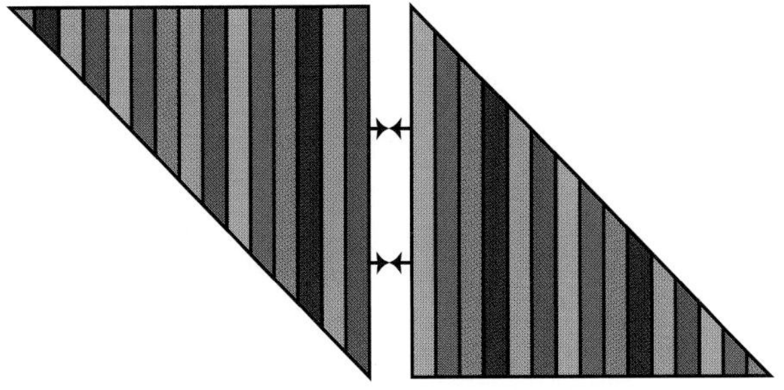

Figure 2–42.

Cut 2½" bias strips from the panel (Figure 2–43).

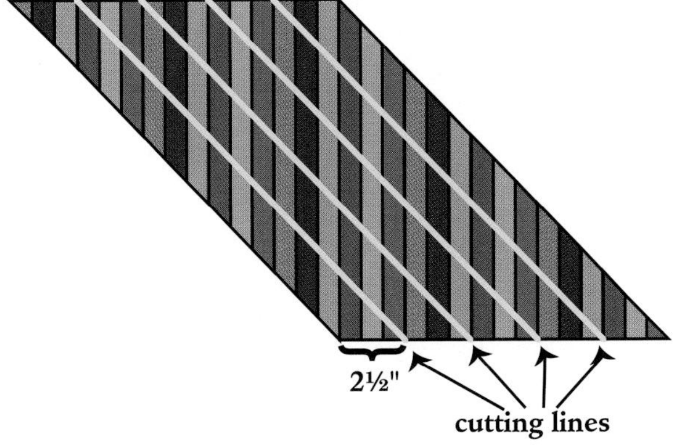

Figure 2–43.

4. Connect the bias strips. Some of the little incomplete strips from each end will have to be removed with a seam ripper, so the strips can be joined in the same color order (Figure 2–44).

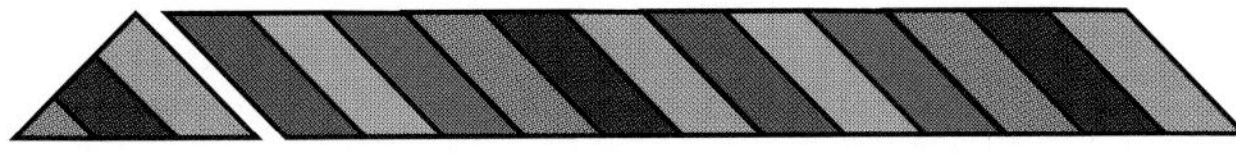

Figure 2–44.

The 15" x 15" panel made for this sample yielded only 72" of binding. Two or three panels will be needed.

Finish the Quilt

Slightly round the corners of the quilt before adding the candy-stripe bias binding. Use your favorite techniques to finish the quilt or see Closing the Circle, page 80, for other finishing ideas.

Mysterious Ovals with Piping

By the author, 38" x 48"

Fabric & Supplies

- 1½ yards of the lighter fabric (includes fabric for the piping)
- 2 yards of the darker fabric (includes border and binding)
- Batting 42" x 52"
- 1⅝ yards backing 42" x 52"
- 2⅓ yards fusible web
- Machine embroidery thread
- Template C for Mysterious Ovals
- 5¾" x 7¾" placement guide
- Chalk marker

Placement Guide

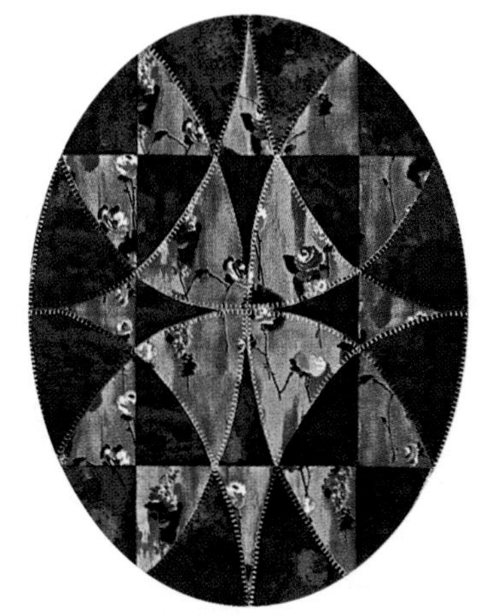

Mysterious Ovals with Piping Project

• Nashville • Wheel of Mystery • Robbing Peter to Pay Paul • Four Leaf Clover • Winding Ways • Robbing Peter to Pay Paul • Four Leaf Clover • Winding Ways • Nashville • Wheel of Mystery •

Cut Blocks, Border, Binding

Cut strips selvage to selvage.

- **From the lighter fabric:**
  Cut twelve 6¼" x 8¼" blocks
  Cut five 1" strips for piping, 180" needed
- **From the darker fabric:**
  Cut thirteen 6¼" x 8¼" blocks
  Cut five 5" x 42" borders
  Cut 2½" strips for binding

Assemble the Quilt Top

1. Piece twenty-five background blocks in a checkerboard pattern, with a rectangle of the darker fabric as the 6¼" x 8¼" center block.

2. Prepare the shapes by tracing Template C on the fusible web twenty-five times. Rough-cut apart. Fuse thirteen fusible web shapes to the remaining lighter fabric and twelve fusible web shapes to the remaining darker fabric. Accurately cut out the shapes (Figure 2–45).

Figure 2–45. Template C on fusible web.

3. Center the 5¾" x 7¾" placement guide on one of the lighter blocks. With the chalk marker, make a mark on the surrounding darker blocks at each ruler arrow. Move the guide, and continue marking all of the remaining darker blocks.

4. Fuse shapes to the pieced background by centering a dark shape on a light block and matching the tips with the chalk marks. Lightly fuse each shape before placing the next one. After all shapes have been lightly fused, firmly press the front and back.

Appliqué Diagrams

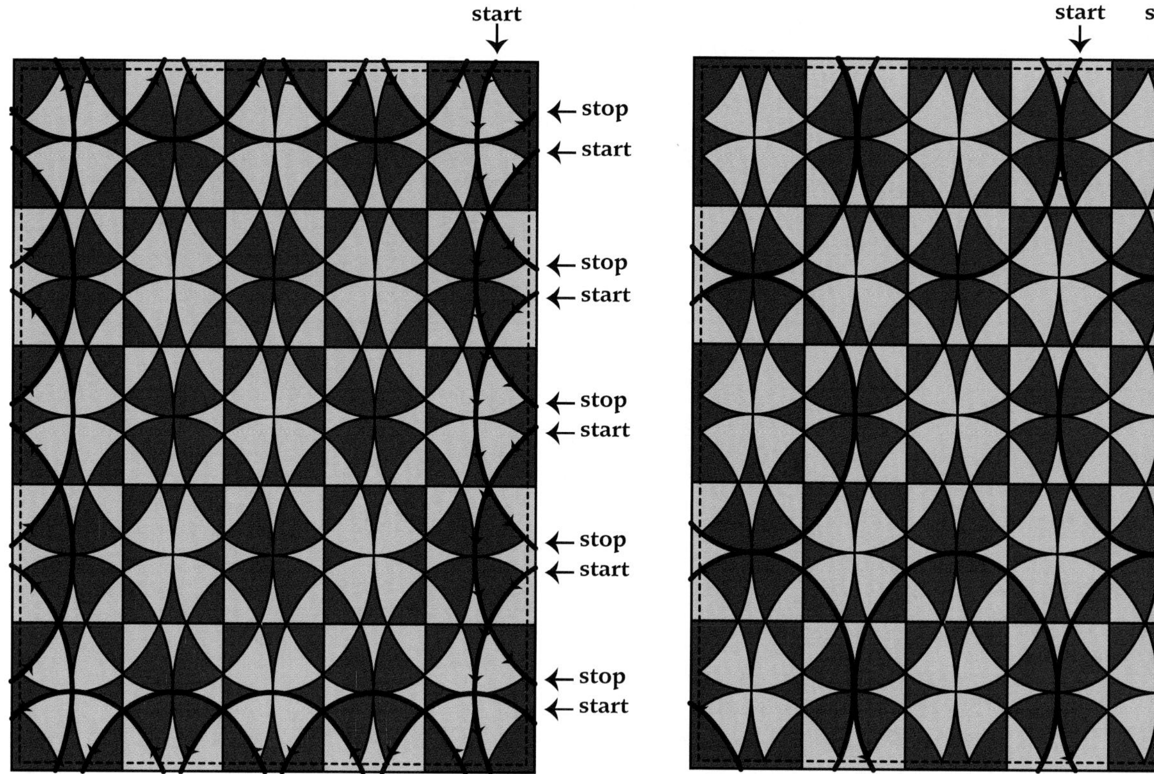

Figure 2–46. Step One.

Figure 2–47. Step Two.

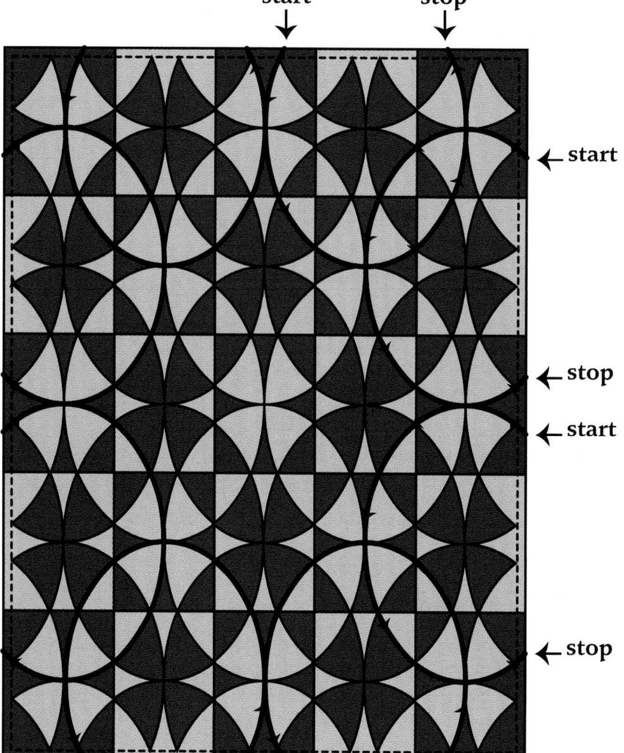

Figure 2–48. Step Three.

Figure 2–49. Step Four.

Appliqué the Shapes

Follow the diagrams above for the stitching sequence for appliqué.

Finish the Quilt

Attach the borders. Layer the backing, batting, and quilt top. Use 2½"-wide binding strips sewn together to bind the edges. Piping can be inserted before binding is added, page 78.

Mysterious Ovals with Self Borders

By the author, 27" x 35"

Fabric & Supplies

- 1¼ yards of the lighter fabric
- 1¼ yards of the darker fabric
- ⅜ yard for binding
- Batting 31" x 39"
- 1¼ yards backing 31" x 39"
- 1½ yards fusible web
- Machine embroidery thread
- Template C for Mysterious Ovals
- 5¾" x 7¾" placement guide
- Chalk marker

Mysterious Ovals with Self Borders Project

• Nashville • Wheel of Mystery • Robbing Peter to Pay Paul • Four Leaf Clover • Winding Ways • Robbing Peter to Pay Paul • Four Leaf Clover • Winding Ways • Nashville • Wheel of Mystery •

Placement Guide

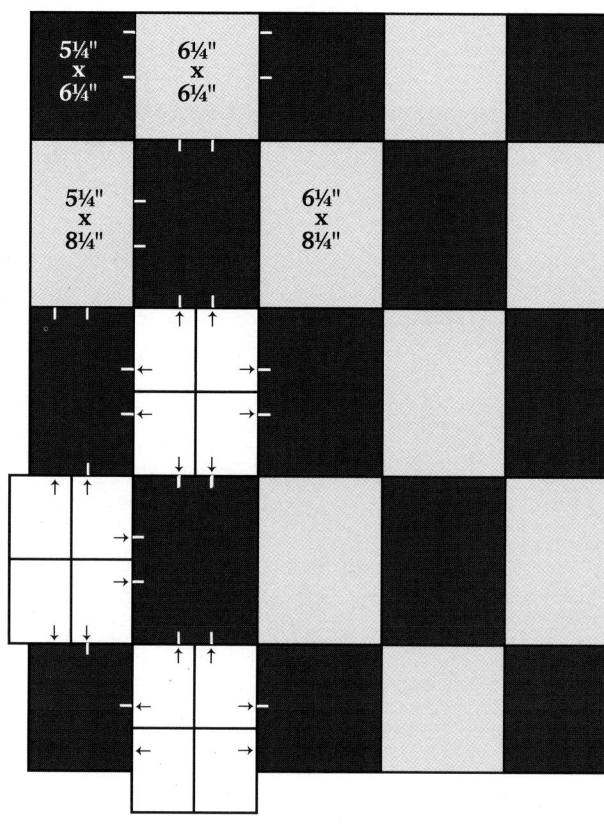

Cut Blocks, Binding

Cut strips selvage to selvage.

- **From the lighter fabric:**
  - Cut four 6¼" x 8¼" blocks
  - Cut four 5¼" x 8¼" blocks
  - Cut four 6¼" x 6¼" blocks
- **From the darker fabric:**
  - Cut five 6¼" x 8¼" blocks
  - Cut two 5¼" x 8¼" blocks
  - Cut four 5¼" x 6¼" blocks
  - Cut two 6¼" x 6¼" blocks
- Cut four 2½" strips to make binding.
- Stack the blocks by size and color.

Assemble the Quilt Top

1. Piece the background blocks following the diagram above for the placement of different sized blocks. Piece in a checkerboard pattern with a rectangle of the darker fabric as the 6¼" x 8¼" center block.

2. Trace Template C on the fusible web sixteen times. Rough-cut apart. Fuse eight fusible web shapes to the remaining lighter fabric and eight fusible web shapes to the remaining darker fabric. Accurately cut out the shapes.

3. Cut selected shapes into parts. Cut these shapes in half: one lighter fabric shape and two darker fabric shapes. Cut these shapes in half the other way: one lighter fabric shape and two darker fabric shapes. Cut one lighter fabric shape into four corner shapes (Figure 2–50).

Figure 2–50. Cut shapes:
(a) Cut one light and two dark shapes in half. (a)

(b) Cut one light shape and two dark shapes in half the other way. (b)

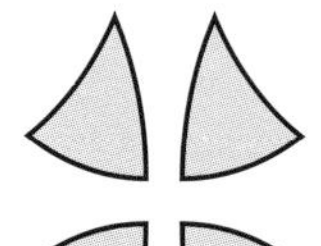

(c) Cut one light shape into quarters. (c)

4. Mark the background blocks with the placement guide. Center the 5¾" x 7¾" guide on one of the lighter blocks. With the chalk marker, make a mark on the surrounding darker fabric blocks at each ruler arrow. Move the ruler, and continue marking all of the remaining darker blocks

5. Fuse the shapes to the pieced background by centering a dark shape on a light block and matching the tips with the chalk marks. Lightly fuse each shape before placing the next one. After all shapes have been lightly fused, firmly press the front and back (Figure 2–51).

Figure 2–51. Whole shapes are fused to full-sized rectangular blocks. Partial shapes are fused to the edge and corner blocks.

Appliqué the Shapes

The diagrams to the right show the stitching sequence for appliqué.

Finish the Quilt

Layer the backing, batting, and quilt top, then quilt around the shapes. Use four 2½"-wide binding strips sewn together, end to end, with diagonal seams to bind the edges.

Appliqué Diagrams

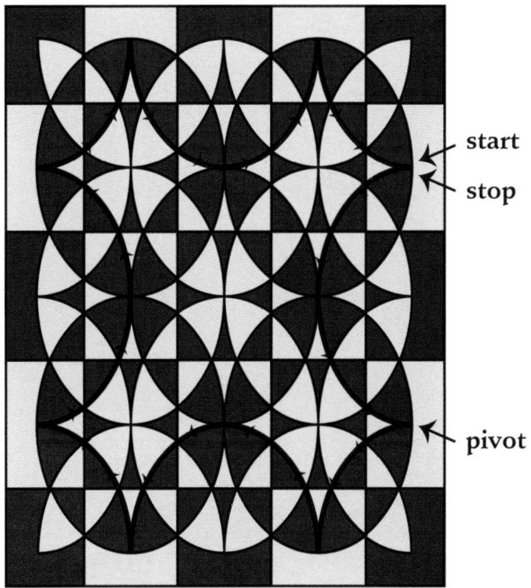

Figure 2–52. Step One.

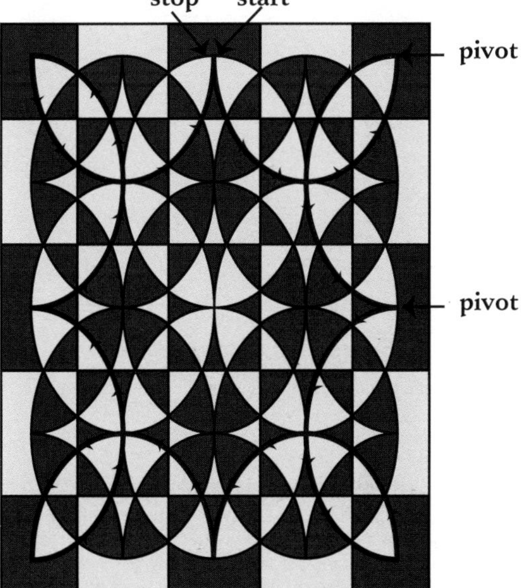

Figure 2–53. Step Two.

Figure 2–54. Step Three.

Spinning Circles variation
by Pennie Horras

Spinning Circles & Simply Circles Project Essentials

The tools, techniques, and construction for Spinning Circles and Simply Circles quilts are basically the same. The exceptions and fabric requirements are detailed with each project.

Fabric Suggestions

Vintage Spinning Circles and Simply Circles quilts were traditionally hand pieced with solid colors for the setting pieces and scraps for the shapes. For the new version of Spinning Circles, the background is a whole piece of fabric on which placement lines can be drawn. Complementary fabrics are used for the shapes.

For Simply Circles, the background can be created from pieced blocks or a whole piece of fabric. Complementary fabrics are used for the shapes. Shapes cut from a variety of fabrics will create a scrappy look.

Both Spinning Circles and Simply Circles quilts can be enlarged simply by selecting a larger background fabric and drawing additional placement lines. For a bed-sized quilt, construct the background by joining two pieces, each the full width (selvage to selvage) of the fabric, and cutting them to the desired length. The seam will be in the vertical center of the backing.

Templates (pages 98 – 101)

- For Spinning Circles, use Template D.
- For Simply Circles, use Templates E and F.

Supplies

- Freezer paper
- Poster board
- Sharp scissors
- Little round sandpaper self-stick grips

To make a template, trace the pattern on a piece of freezer paper 1" larger all around than the pattern. Iron-fuse the paper to a piece of poster board. The paper will stick long enough for you to cut along the traced lines. Label the template with the corresponding letter and stick little sandpaper grips on the back.

Assembling the Quilt

1. Straight lines will be drawn on the background. For a nice finish to draw on (prewashed or not), spray size the fabric, let it dry, and press. Test some markers. A white chalk roller marker is a good choice for just about every color except the very lightest. A quilter's pencil or a #2 pencil is good. Do not use permanent markers. Do the drawing on a flat surface. You can use a cutting mat.

2. To prepare the shapes, use a fine-tipped permanent marker to trace the template on the paper side of the fusible web, in rows across the width of the web. Leave a ¼" space between the tracings.

3. A 17"-wide piece of fusible web should yield seven Spinning Circles shapes, six whole Simply Circles shapes, or seven Simply Circles half-shapes.

4. Rough-cut the rows apart. If several of the appliquéd shapes are going to be cut from the same fabric, the rows of shapes traced on the fusible web can be fused to one large piece of the chosen fabric. If the appliquéd shapes are going to be cut from multiple fabrics, the shapes traced on fusible web can be cut apart and fused to the desired fabrics. After fusing to the fabrics, cut out shapes along traced lines.

5. To fuse the shapes to the prepared background, first determine how you want different colors arranged by randomly placing the shapes on the background and observing. The shapes are centered and fused over all of the drawn lines or seams. The tips will meet and snug up to each other at the intersections. It is best if they do *not* overlap. If they do, it means the shapes are a little long. Trim a scant bit of fabric off the tips until they meet correctly. If a shape is short or does not meet at all, try another one or shift them slightly. Usually the decorative stitches will cover any small gaps.

Appliquéing the Quilt Top

It's a good idea to make a practice block with the fabrics selected for the quilt. Test different embroidery stitches for the appliqué to find the one that works best and experiment with stabilizers. Apply stabilizer, if necessary, to the back of the pieced top.

Appliqué the shapes in sequence, following the diagrams shown with the project. Machine appliqué for Spinning Circles and Simply Circles is done in rows. The inside rows of shapes are appliquéd first, and the outside rows of shapes are stitched last. Each row is appliquéd twice, once on each side.

To appliqué, stitch one side of a row and then the other. On most tops, stop and pivot at the end of the row and continue stitching the other side. If tops are too large to pivot, start appliquéing again at the beginning of the row. After the rows in one direction are appliquéd, tie off and trim the threads before continuing.

Projects with Pivots – The sewing sequence diagrams in each project show where to pivot at the end of stitching rows. Use your own techniques or try these suggestions.

For directional appliqué stitches:

1. Stop stitching at the pivot point with the needle down to your right (at its right swing).
2. Raise the presser foot.
3. Rotate the quilt top.
4. Lower the presser foot and continue stitching.

For non-directional appliqué stitches:

1. Stop stitching at the pivot point with the needle down.
2. Raise the presser foot.
3. Rotate the quilt top.
4. Lower the presser foot.
5. Raise the needle.
6. Raise the presser foot.
7. Adjust the quilt top slightly in either direction to align the stitches correctly.
8. Lower the presser foot, and continue stitching.

Finishing the Quilt

Press the quilt top after the appliqué is done. Cut off the selvages, if any. Square the quilt top an equal distance from the appliquéd shapes. Find the narrowest distance and use that as the measurement for all four sides.

Note: This finishing technique does *not* pertain to the Simply Circles I and Simply Circles II projects.

Tips & Hints

Fusible Web
For illustrations on preparing shapes with fusible web, see page 15 in the Project Essentials for Mysterious Circles and Ovals.

Steering the Stitching
The stitching will flow along smoothly once you start to machine appliqué. It's just like driving a car – look ahead a little and follow the curves.

Go with the Flow
If you feel the stitching flows better, you can cross over from one edge of the row to the other edge at intersections when using a non-directional stitch. If the stitch is directional and requires mirror imaging when the stitching line crosses from one shape to the next, see Starting the Circle, page 8.

Spinning Circles I

By the author, 31" x 33"

Fabric & Supplies

- 1 yard total for the appliqué shapes, all one fabric or assorted. If using assorted fabrics, allow 2½" x 7½" for each appliqué shape.
- 1¼ yards background. Choose a fabric on which drawn placement lines will show.
- ½ yard binding.
  Note: If the same fabric is used for the background and the binding, 1⅝ yards will be needed.
- Batting 35" x 37"
- 1⅛ yards backing 35" x 37"
- 1¾ yards fusible web
- Machine embroidery thread
- Template D for Spinning Circles
- 6" x 24" ruler with 60° lines
- A marker that will show on the background fabric.

Spinning Circles I Project

• Joseph's Coat • Peeled Orange • Daisy Chain • Daisy Chain • Joseph's Coat • Peeled Orange • Joseph's Coat • Peeled Orange • Daisy Chain Daisy Chain • Joseph's Coat • Peeled Orange • Joseph's Coat • Peeled Orange • Daisy Chain Daisy Chain • Joseph's Coat • Peeled Orange • Joseph's Coat • Peeled Orange • Daisy Chain

Placement Guide I

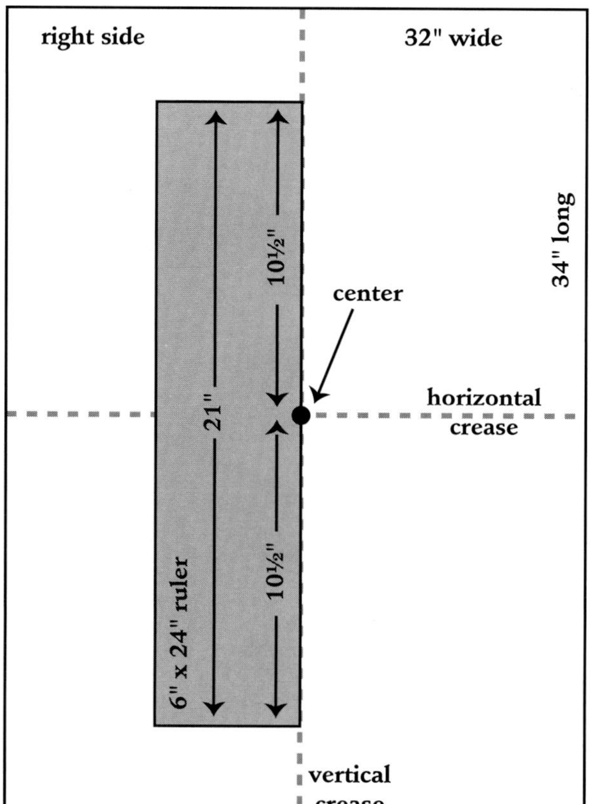

Prepare the Shapes

Trace Template D on the fusible web forty-nine times. Fuse the shapes to the desired fabric or fabrics and cut out accurately.

Prepare the Background Fabric

1. Cut a 32" x 34" rectangle. To find the center, fold the fabric, right sides together with the edges aligned, and press a center vertical crease. Refold and press a center horizontal crease.

2. Draw the placement lines for the shapes on the right side of the background fabric. When drawing the lines, be as accurate as possible. Use the 6" x 24" ruler for all of the measuring steps and draw with a marker that will show well on the fabric. There will be no lines drawn on the horizontal crease. Use it as a measuring guide.

3. Draw a 21" line directly on the vertical crease. It will measure 10½" from the horizontal crease in both directions. See Placement Guide I.

Spinning Circles variation
by Dianne Sullivan, 32" x 47½"

Placement Guide II

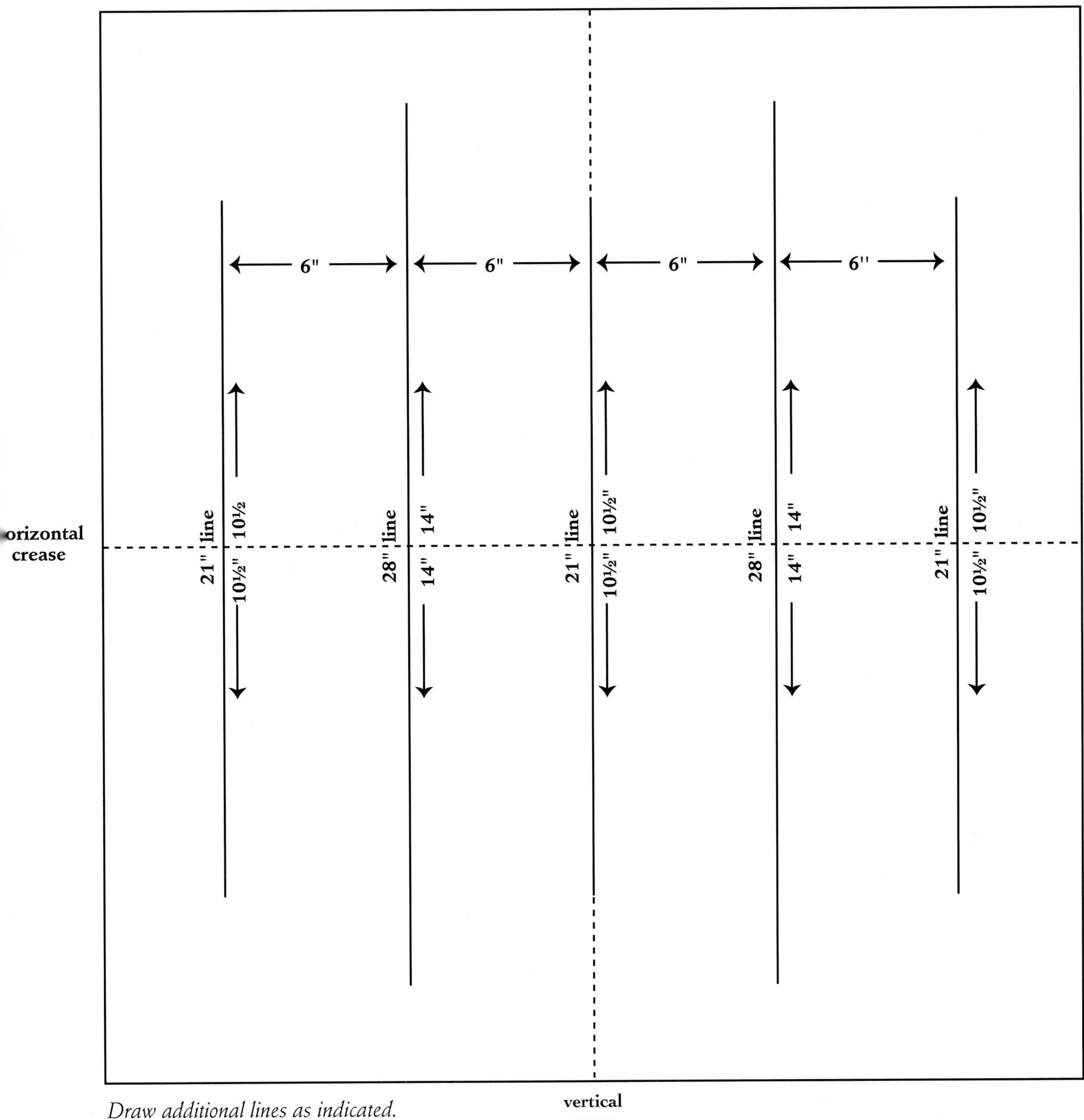

Draw additional lines as indicated.

4. Draw one 28" vertical line on each side of the 21" center vertical line. Place the new lines 6" (the exact width of the 6" x 24" ruler) away from the center line. These lines will measure 14" from the horizontal crease in both directions. Then, draw one 21" line 6" away from each of the 28" lines. These lines will measure 10½" from the horizontal crease in both directions. There will be five lines.

Placement Guide III

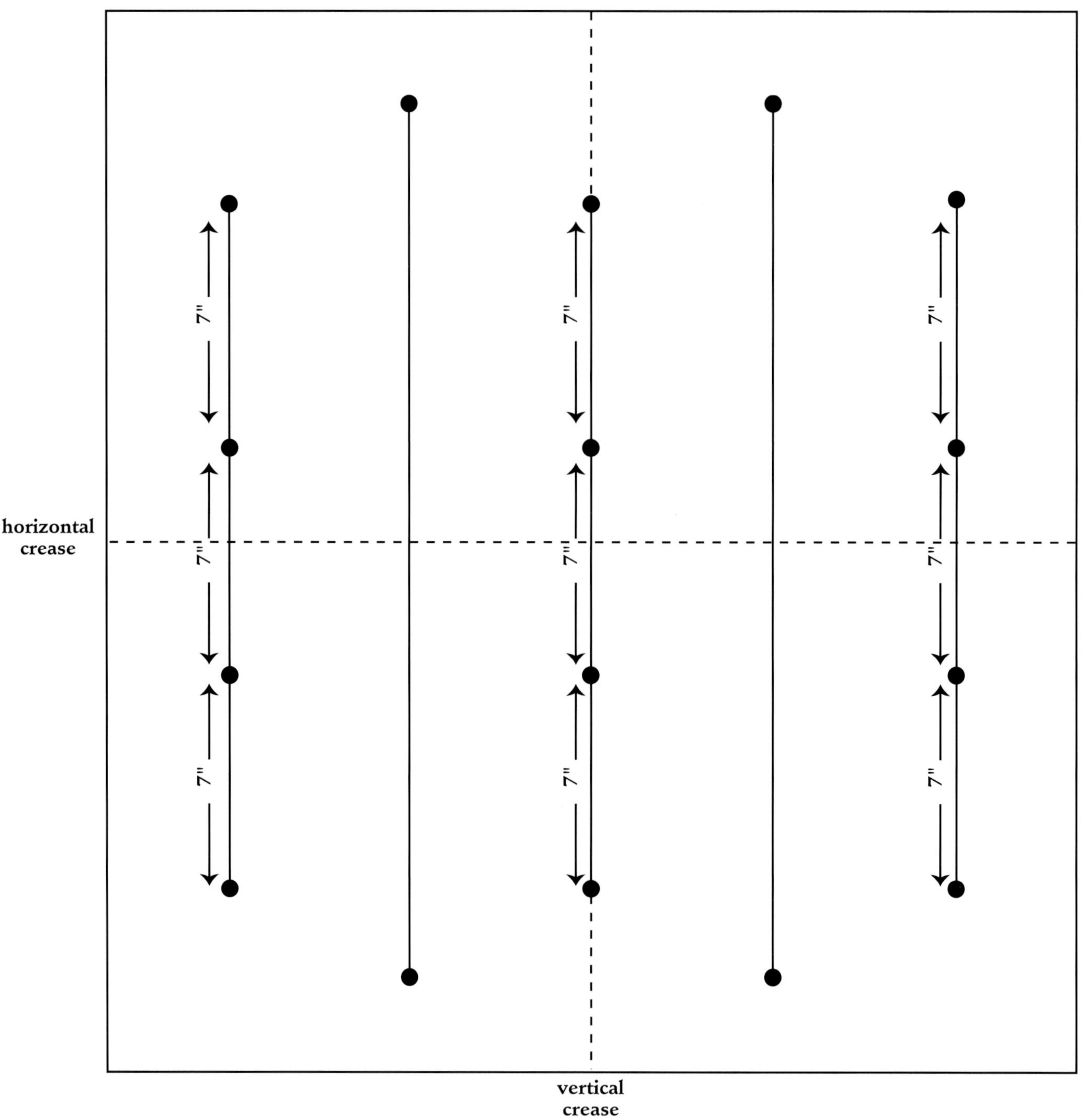

Mark the 21" lines with dots every 7" and at both ends.
Mark dots on the ends of the remaining lines

5. On the center and outside 21" vertical lines, mark dots every 7", starting at the ends of the lines. Mark dots on the ends of the 28" lines (See Placement Guide III above).

6. Check the accuracy of the dots by laying the ruler's 60° line on a vertical line on the fabric with the ruler's long edges lined up with the dots. Because the fabric is supple, there will be slight variations in the marking (Figure 2–55).

7. Connect the dots by drawing 60° lines. Draw all the lines in one direction (Figure 2–55).

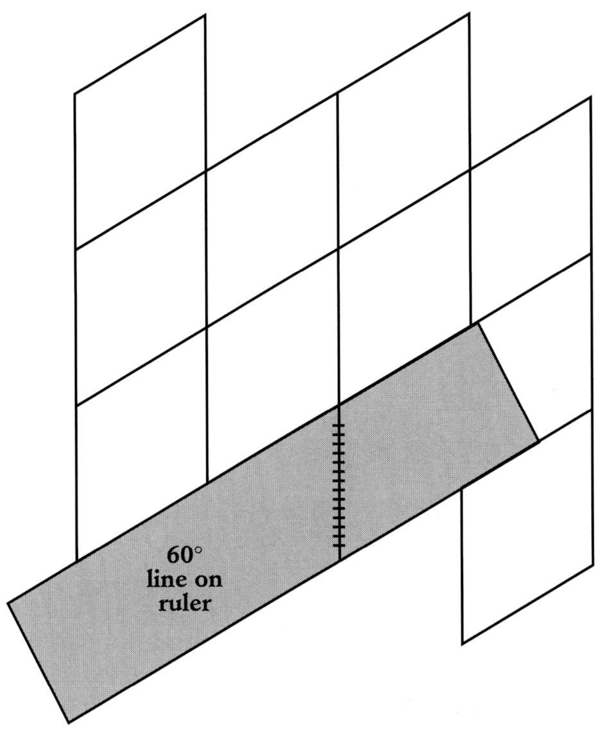

Figure 2–55. With the ruler as a straight edge, draw 60° lines connecting the dots.

8. Draw the lines in the other direction. These lines will intersect the first lines, forming the centers of the Spinning Circles. The distance between the intersections is 7" (Figure 2–56).

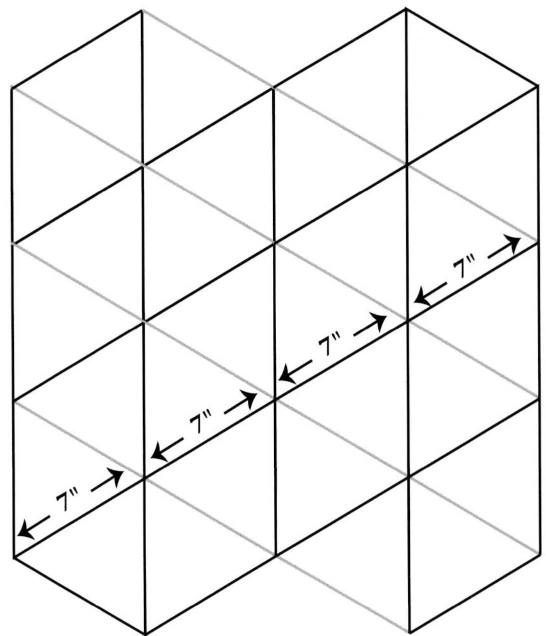

Figure 2–56. Move the ruler and connect the dots with lines in the other direction.

Fuse the shapes

Begin fusing the shapes to the prepared background by placing and lightly fusing the shapes one row across at a time. After all the shapes have been lightly fused, firmly press on the front and back (Figure 2–57).

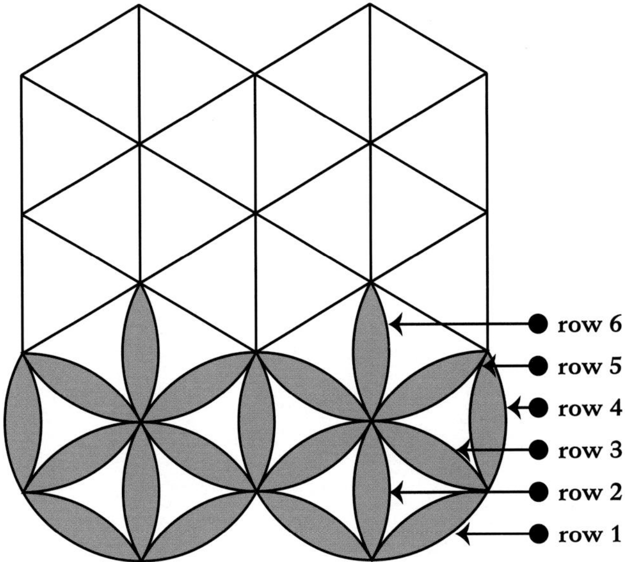

Figure 2–57. Fuse the shapes, moving across the fabric in horizontal rows.

Appliqué the Shapes

The diagrams on page 56 (Figure 2–58 through 2–61) show the stitching sequence for appliqué. Continue the sequence shown to complete all rows.

Finish the Quilt Top

Press the quilt top after the appliqué is done. Layer the backing, batting, and quilt top.

Square the quilt top an equal distance from the appliquéd shapes.

Finish the Quilt

Use binding strips sewn together, end to end, with diagonal seams to bind the edges. See Closing the Circle, page 81, for professional binding tips.

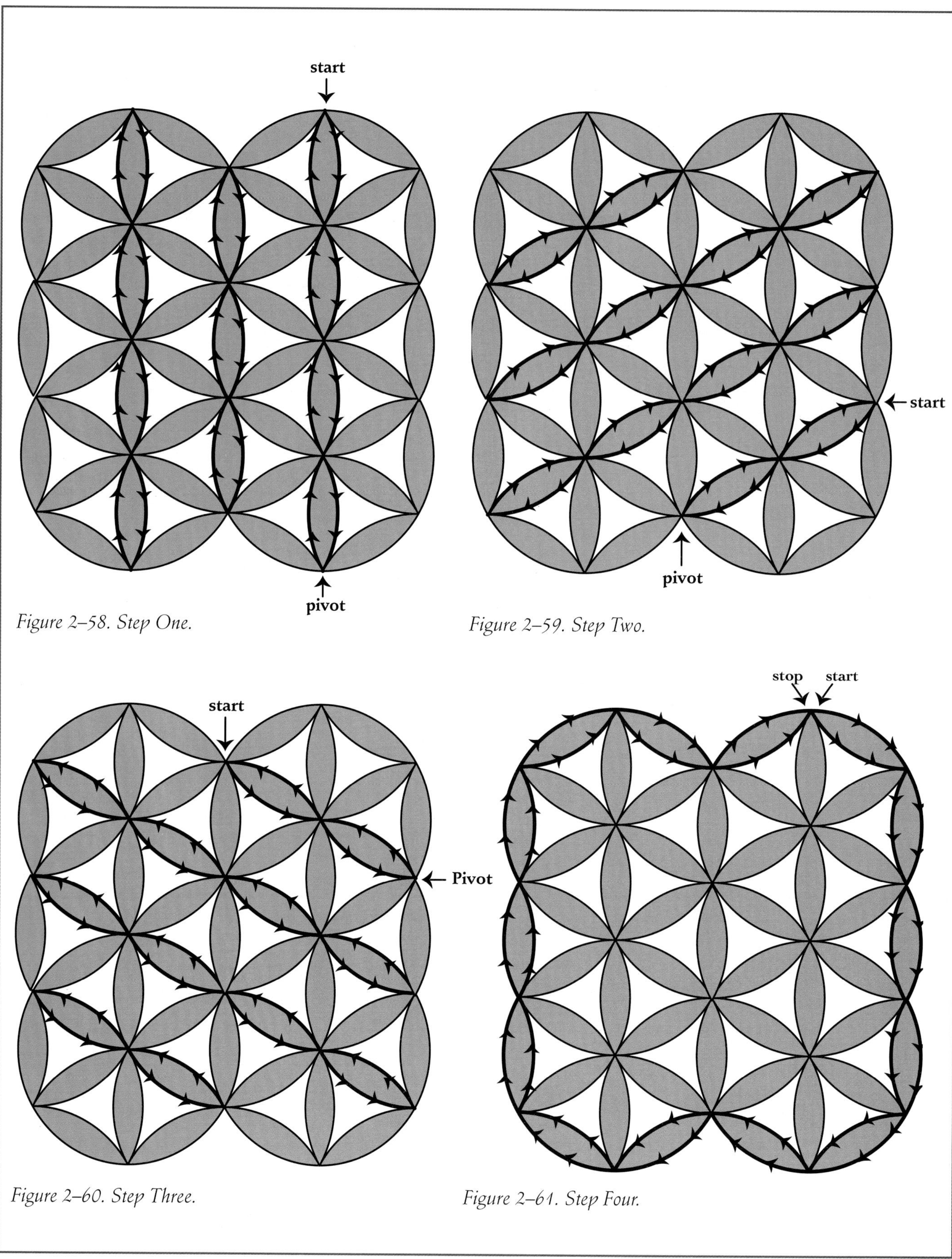

Figure 2–58. Step One.

Figure 2–59. Step Two.

Figure 2–60. Step Three.

Figure 2–61. Step Four.

Spinning Circles II

By the author, 42" x 47"

Fabric & Supplies

- 1⅔ yards for the appliqué shapes, all one fabric or assorted.
- 1⅝ yards for the background. Choose a fabric on which drawn placement lines will show.
- ½ yard for the binding.

Note: If the same fabric is used for the background and the binding, 2 yards will be needed.

- Batting 46" x 51"
- 3 yards of backing 46" x 51"
  (2 panels - 23" x 51")
- 4 yards fusible web
- Machine embroidery thread
- Template D for Spinning Circles
- 6" x 24" ruler with 60° lines
- A marker that will show on the background fabric.

Spinning Circle II Project

• Daisy Chain • Joseph's Coat • Peeled Orange • Joseph's Coat • Peeled Orange • Daisy Chain • Peeled Orange • Daisy Chain • Joseph's Coat • Daisy Chain • Joseph's Coat • Peeled Orange • Joseph's Coat • Peeled Orange • Daisy Chain

Placement Guide I

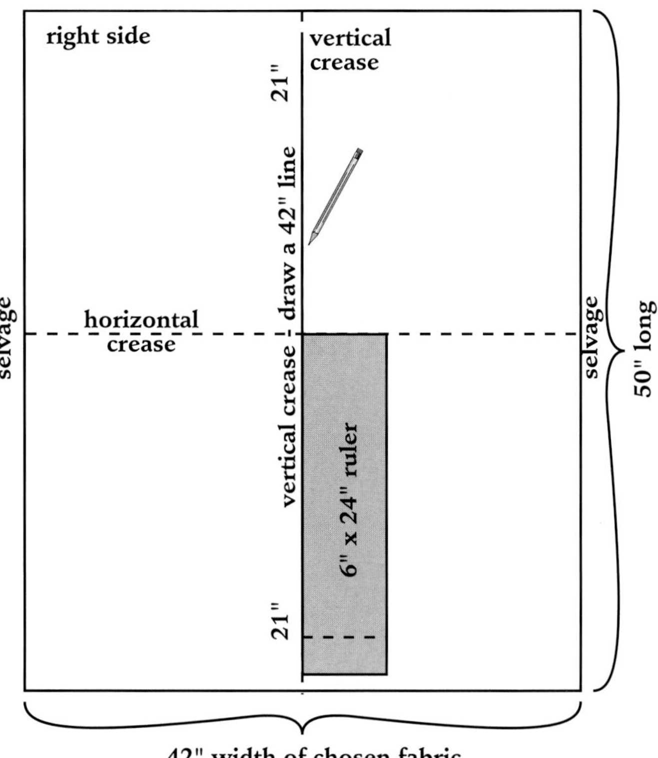

Prepare the Shapes.

1. Trace Template D on the fusible web 110 times. Fuse the shapes to the desired fabric or fabrics, and accurately cut them out.

Prepare the Background

Do not cut off the selvages, they will be removed later.

2. Cut the fabric to the correct length, and find the center. First, press the fabric and cut the length to 50". Leave the width of the fabric as it is. In this project, the sample is 42" x 50". Each project may vary, depending on the width of the fabric. To find the center, fold the fabric, right sides together with the edges lined up and press a centered vertical crease, then refold and press a centered horizontal crease (See Placement Guide).

3. Draw the placement lines for the shapes. Lines are drawn on the right side of the fabric. When drawing the placement lines on the background fabric, be as accurate as possible. Use a 6" x 24" ruler for all of the measuring steps and draw with a marker that will show on the fabric. There will be no lines drawn on the horizontal crease. Use it as a measuring guide.

4. Draw a 42" line centered on the vertical crease. It will measure 21" from the horizontal crease in both directions.

5. Draw a 35" vertical line on each side of the center 42" line. Place the new lines 6" (the exact width of the 6 x 24" ruler) away from the 21" center line. These lines will measure 17½" from the horizontal crease in both directions. Continue drawing the remaining lines, referring to Placement Guide II for line length (page 59).

All templates are on pages 98 - 101.

Placement Guide II

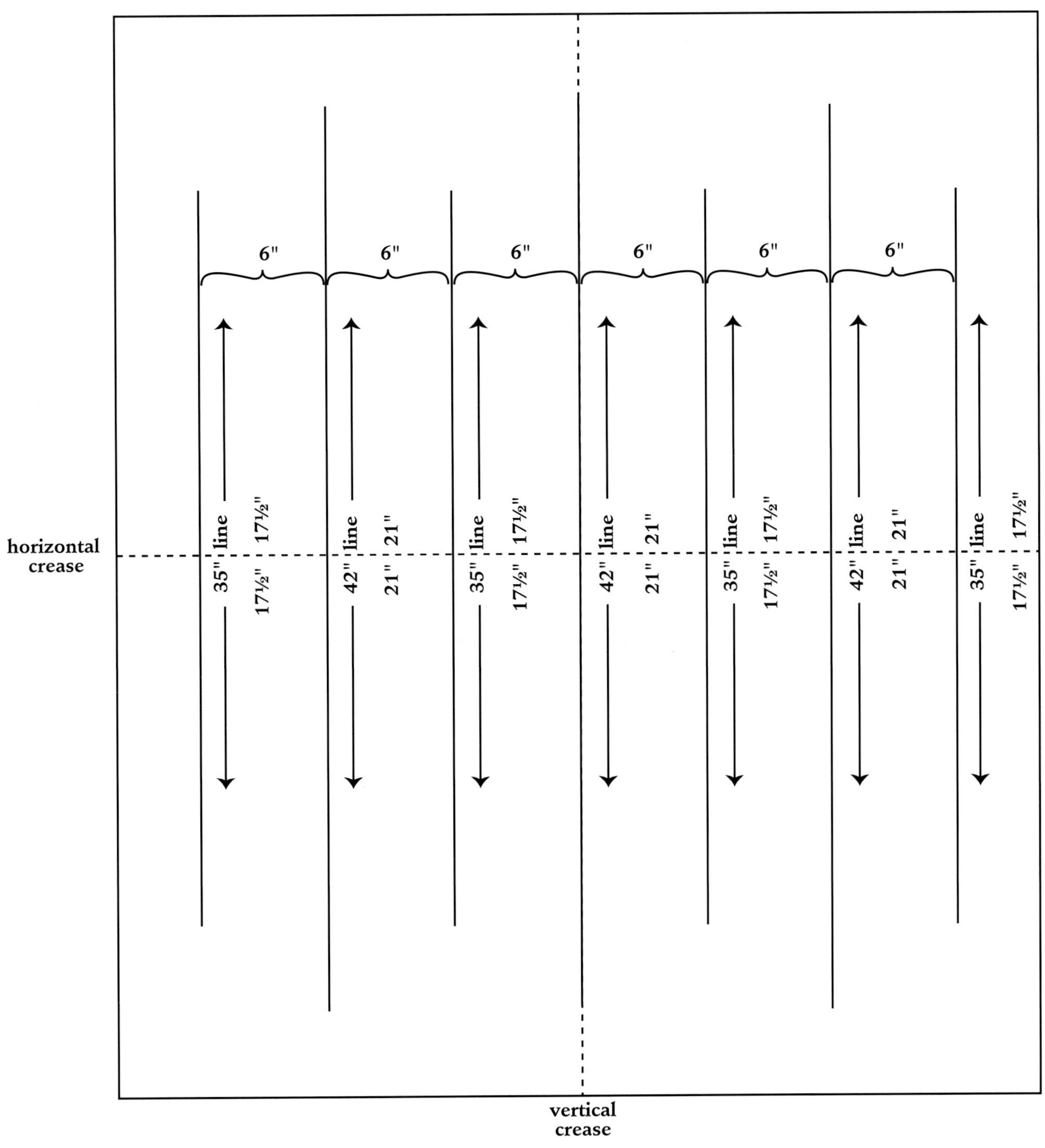

Draw additional lines as indicated.

Placement Guide III

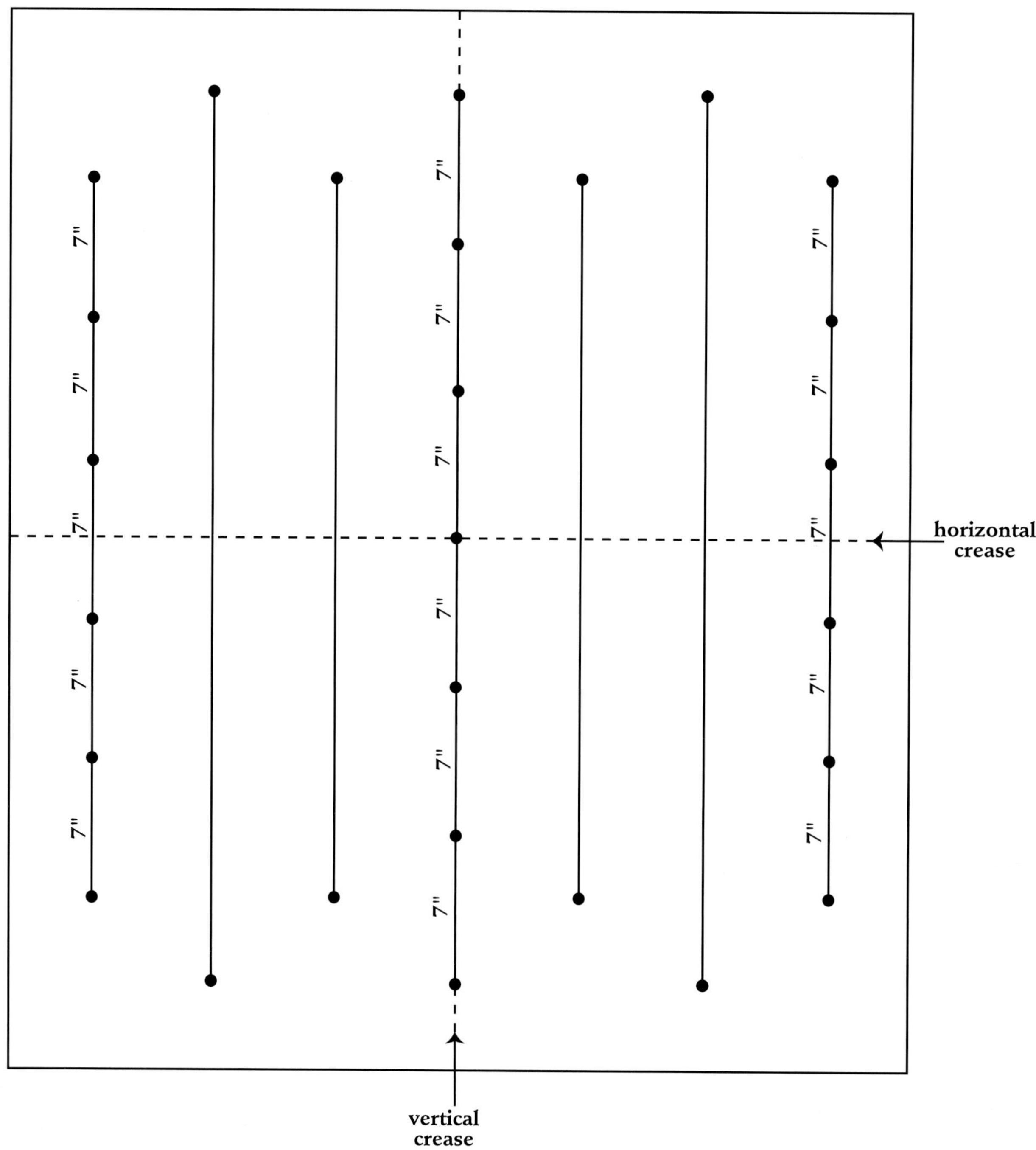

Mark the center 42" and the outside 35" vertical lines with dots every 7" and at both ends. Mark dots on the ends of the remaining lines.

6. On the center 42" and the outside 35" vertical lines, mark dots every 7", starting at the ends of the lines. Mark dots on the ends of the remaining lines, see above.

7. Check the accuracy of the dots by laying the ruler's 60° line on a vertical line on the fabric with the ruler's long edges lined up with the dots. Because the fabric is supple, there will be slight variations in the markings (Figure 2–62).

Connect the dots by drawing 60° lines. Draw all the lines in one direction (Figure 2–62).

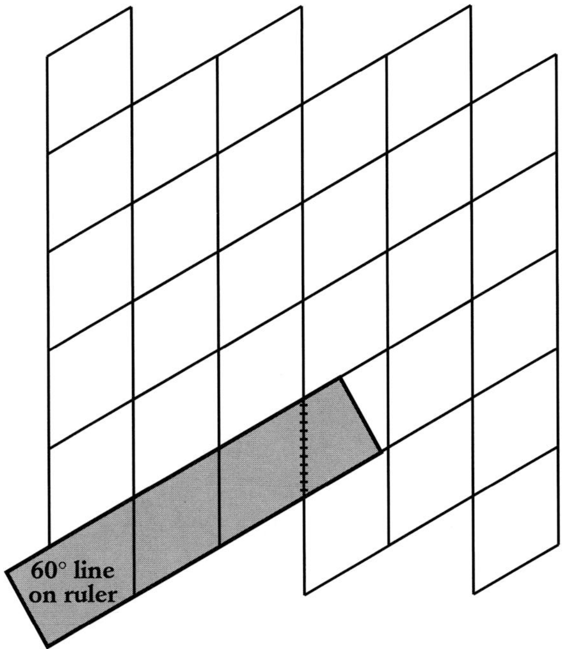

Figure 2–62. With the ruler as a straight edge, draw 60° lines connecting the dots.

8. Draw the lines in the other direction. These lines will intersect the other lines, forming the centers of the Spinning Circles. The distance between the intersections is 7" (Figure 2–63).

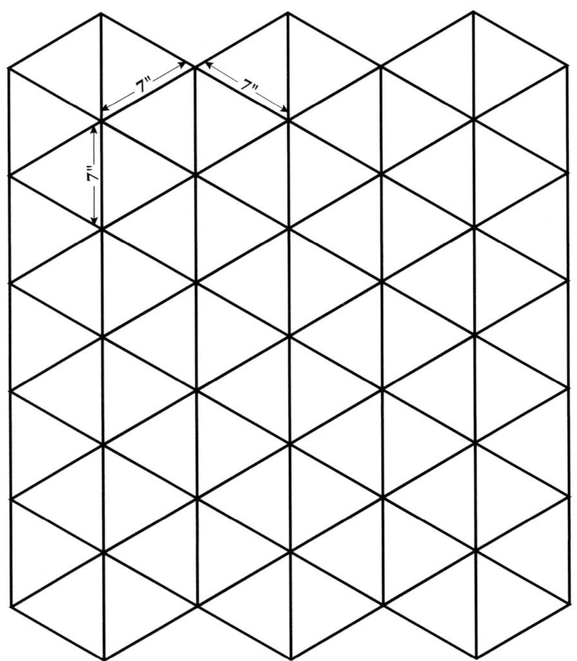

Figure 2–63. Move the ruler, and connect the dots with lines in the other direction.

Fuse the Shapes

9. Begin fusing the shapes to the prepared background by placing and lightly fusing the shapes one row across at a time. After all of the shapes are lightly fused, firmly press the top and back (Figure 2–64).

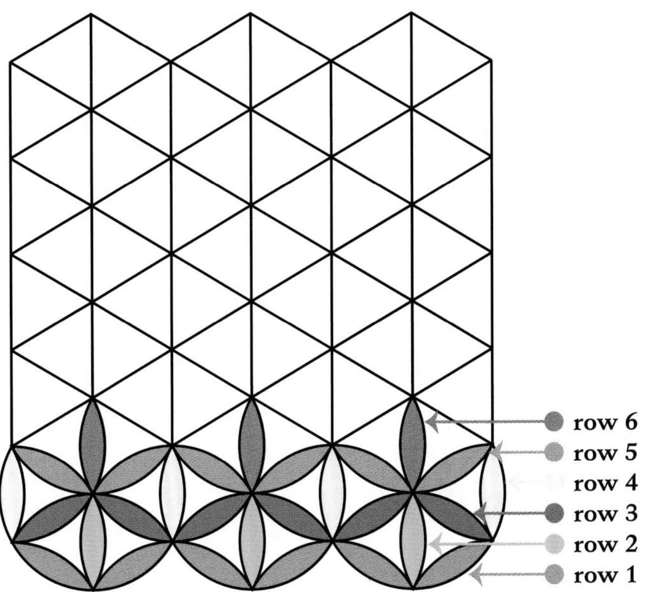

Figure 2–64. Fuse the shapes, moving across the fabric in horizontal rows.

Appliqué the Shapes

The diagrams on the next page show the stitching sequence for appliqué (Figures 2–65 through 2–68). Continue the sequence shown to complete all rows.

Finish the Quilt Top

Press the quilt top after the appliqué is done. Quilt the top. Square the quilt top an equal distance from the appliquéd shapes. Find the narrowest distance and use that as the measurement for all four sides.

Finish the Quilt

Use your favorite techniques, or see Closing the Circle, page 81, for finishing ideas.

Appliqué Diagrams

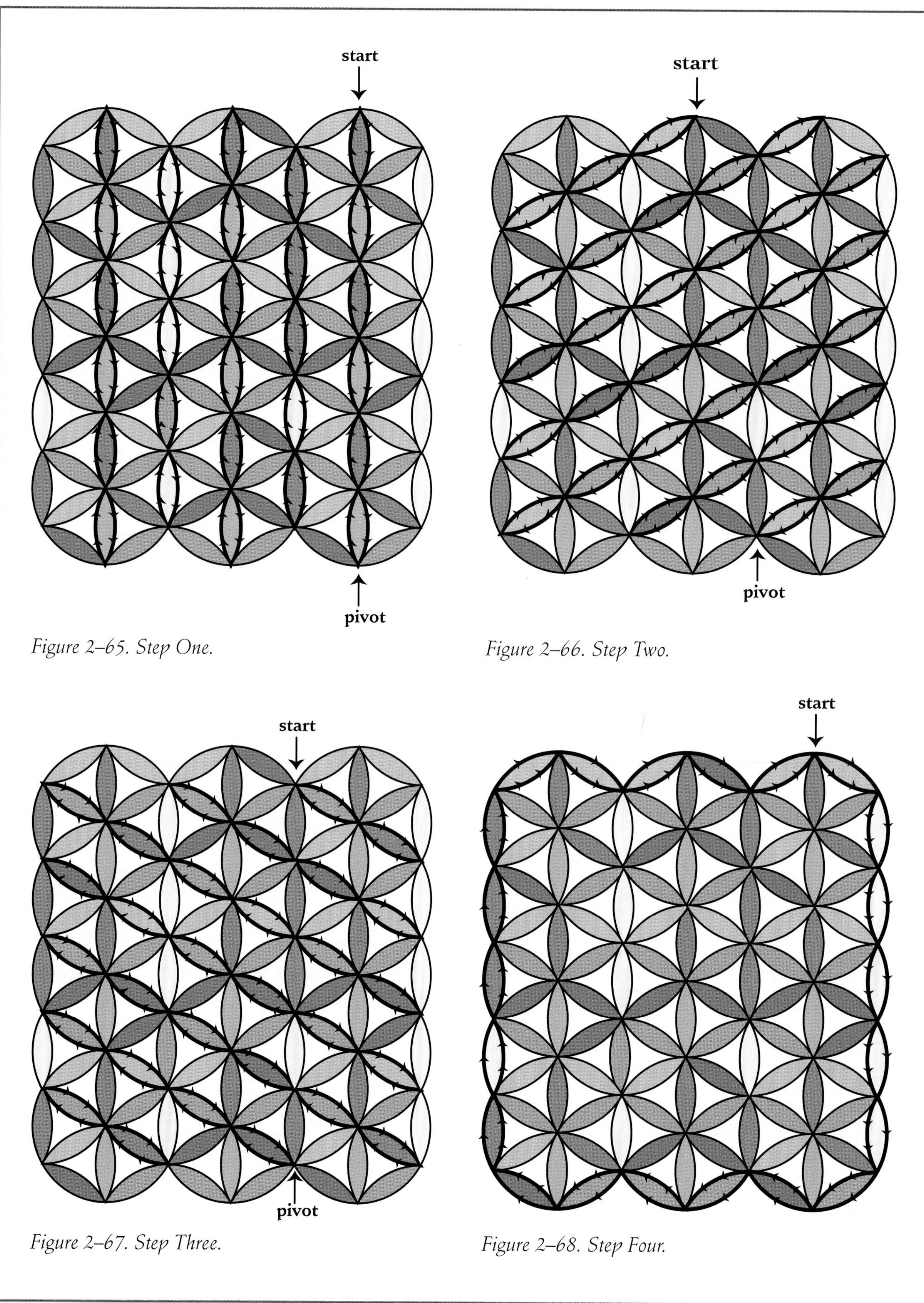

Figure 2–65. Step One.

Figure 2–66. Step Two.

Figure 2–67. Step Three.

Figure 2–68. Step Four.

Simply Circles I

By the author, 30" x 30"

Fabric & Supplies

- ¾ yard total for the appliqué shapes, all one fabric or assorted. If using assorted fabrics, allow 3" x 6½" for each whole shape and 2" x 6½" for each half shape.
- 1⅛ yards for the background. Choose a fabric on which drawn placement lines will show.
- ⅜ yard for the binding.
- Batting 34" x 34"
- 1 yard of backing, 34" x 34"
- 1⅓ yards fusible web
- Machine embroidery thread
- Templates E and F for Simply Circles
- 6" x 24" ruler
- A marker that will show on the background fabric.

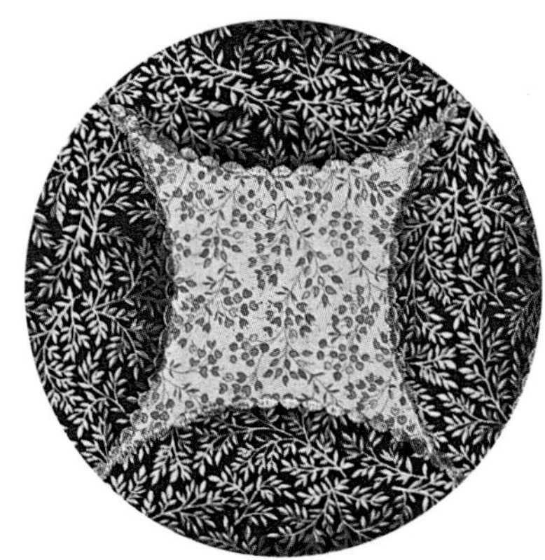

Simply Circles I Project

• Tea Leaf • Compass • Lover's Knot • Lafayette Orange Peel • Circle Upon Circle • Bay Leaf • Pin Cushion • Whispering Leaves • Save a Piece • Melon Patch • Flower Petals • Circle Upon Circle

Placement Guide I

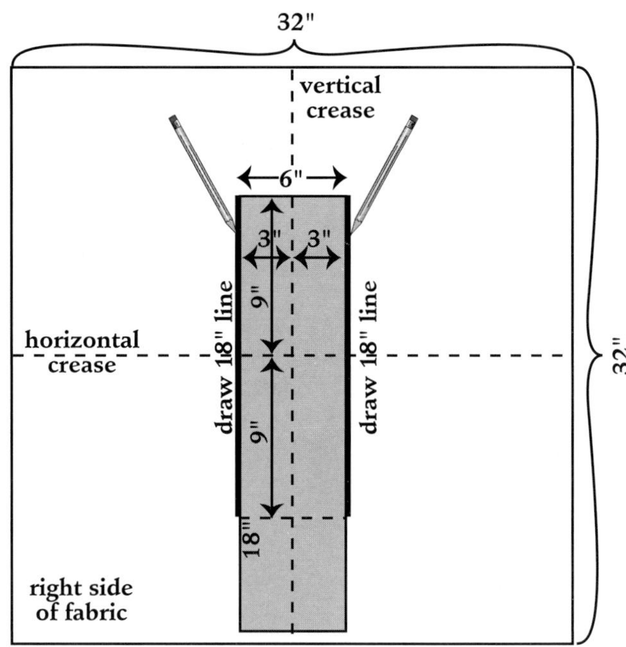

Position the ruler's lengthwise 3" line on the vertical crease with the 9" crosswise line on the center of the creases, and mark 18" lines on both sides of the ruler.

Prepare the Shapes

Trace Template E on the fusible web twenty-four times. Trace Template F on the fusible web twenty times. Fuse the shapes to the desired fabric or fabrics and accurately cut out.

Prepare the Background

1. Cut the background in a 32" x 32" square. To find the center, fold the fabric, right sides together with the edges lined up, and press a center vertical crease. Refold and press a center horizontal crease.

2. Draw placement lines on the right side of the fabric as accurately as possible. Use the 6" x 24" ruler for all of the measuring steps and draw with a marker that will show on the fabric. There will be no lines drawn on the creases. Use them as measuring guides.

3. Center the ruler's lengthwise 3" line on the vertical crease with the crosswise 9" line on the exact center of the creases. Draw 18" lines on both sides of the ruler. The lines will measure 9" from the horizontal crease in both directions. Refer to Placement Guide I at top.

Placement Guide II

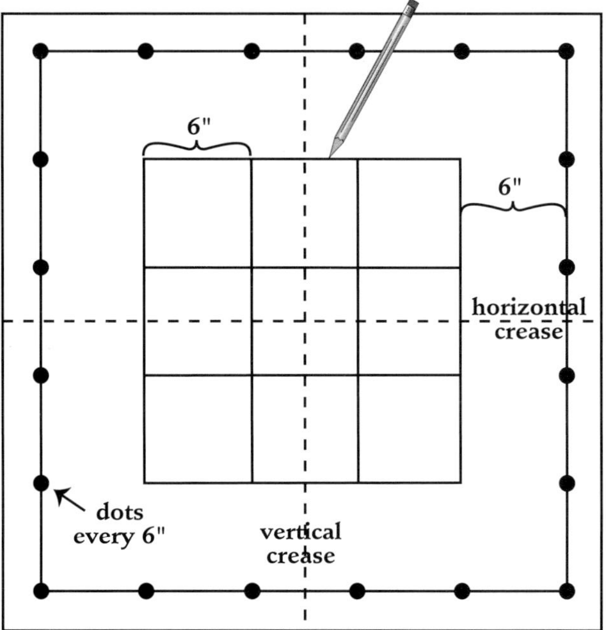

Placement Guide III

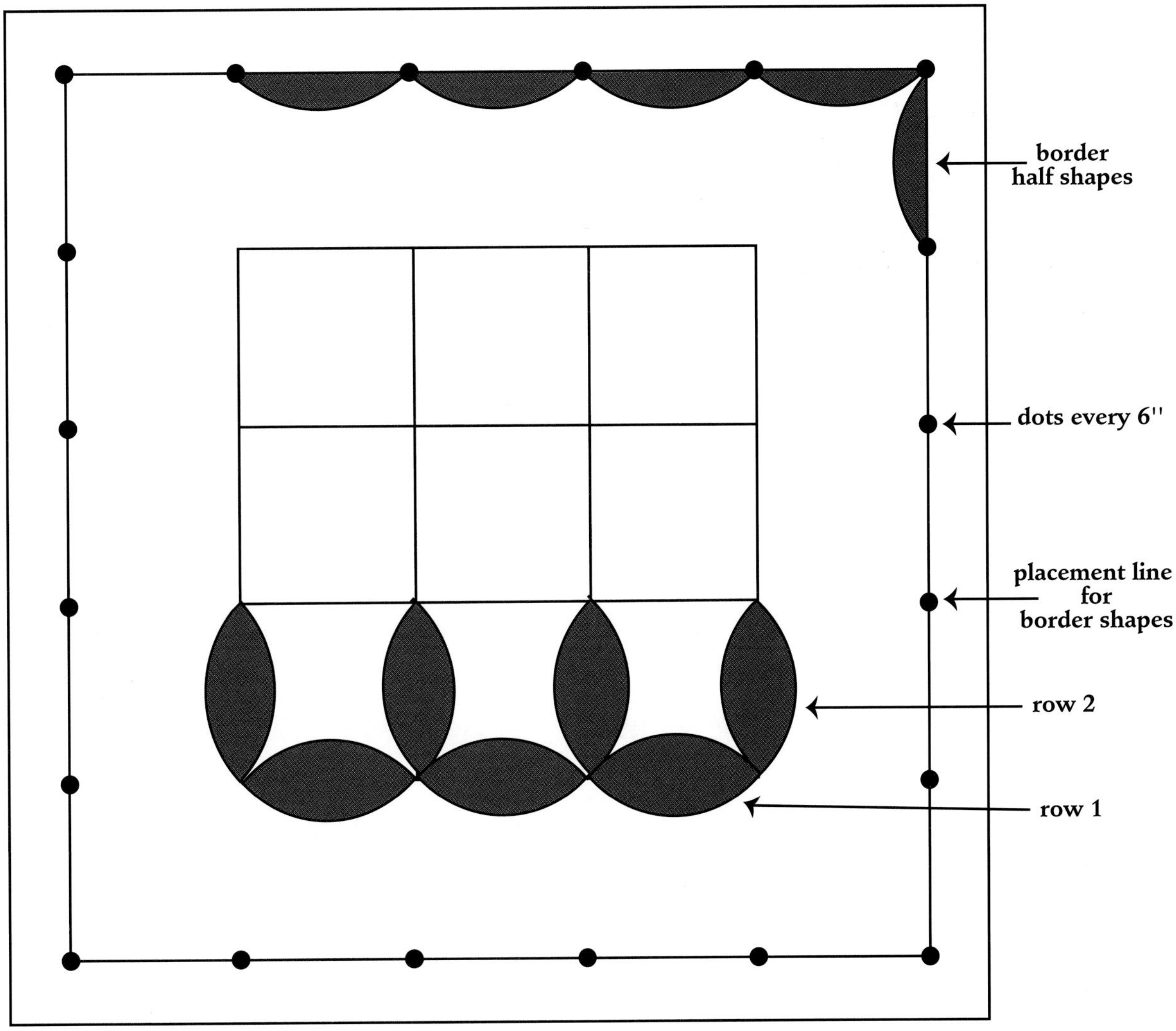

border half shapes
dots every 6"
placement line for border shapes
row 2
row 1

Fuse the whole shapes, moving across the grid lines in horizontal rows. Fuse the border half shapes on the outer placement line.

4. Using the 6" width of the ruler, continue drawing the remaining 18" vertical lines. Align the ruler on the horizontal crease, and repeat the process to create horizontal lines, forming a grid. Draw lines for the border shapes 6" from the outside lines of the grid. Mark the border placement lines with dots every 6". Refer to Placement Guide II.

Fuse the Shapes

Begin fusing the shapes to the prepared background by placing and lightly fusing the shapes one row across at a time. The border half shapes go between the 6" dots and may slightly overlap each other. After all of the shapes are lightly fused, firmly press the top and the back. Refer to Placement Guide III, above.

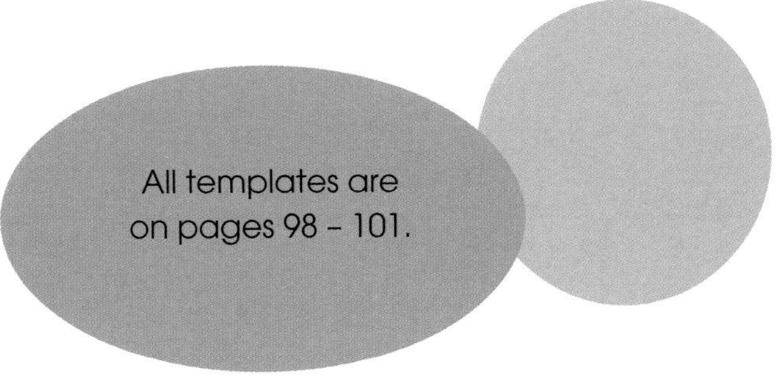

Appliqué Diagrams

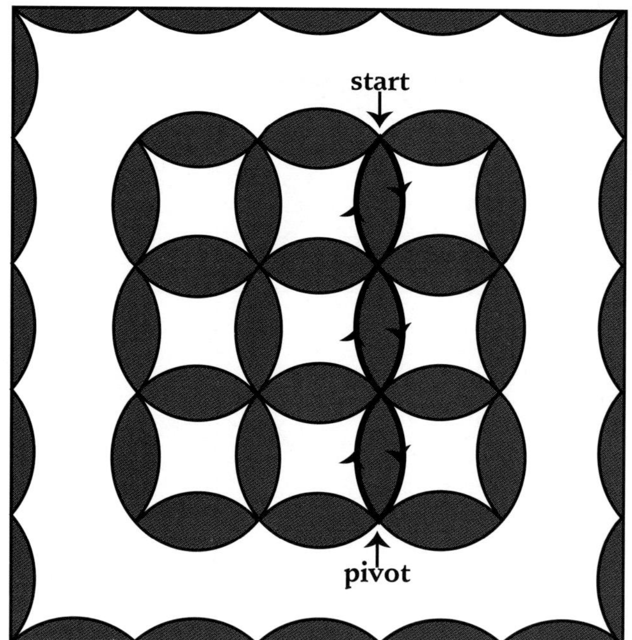

Figure 2–69. Step One.

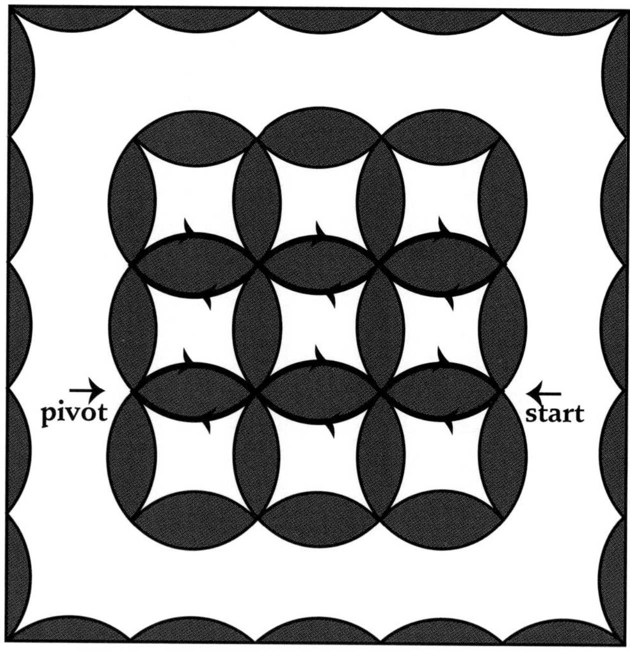

Figure 2–70. Step Two.

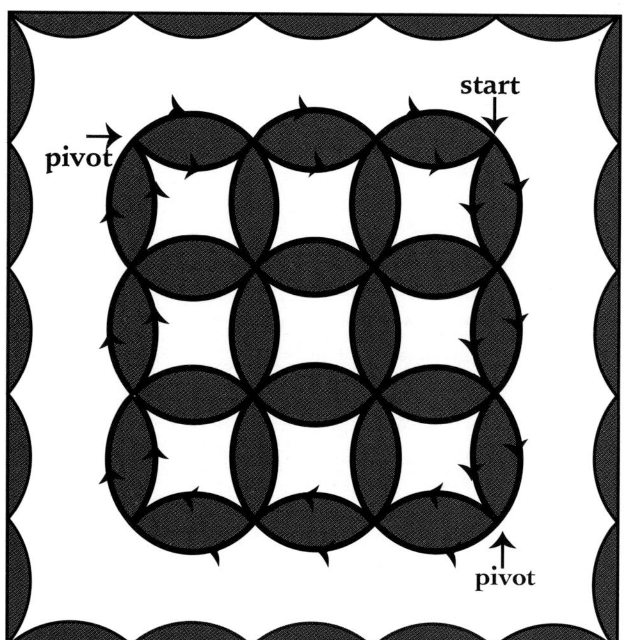

Figure 2–71. Step Three.

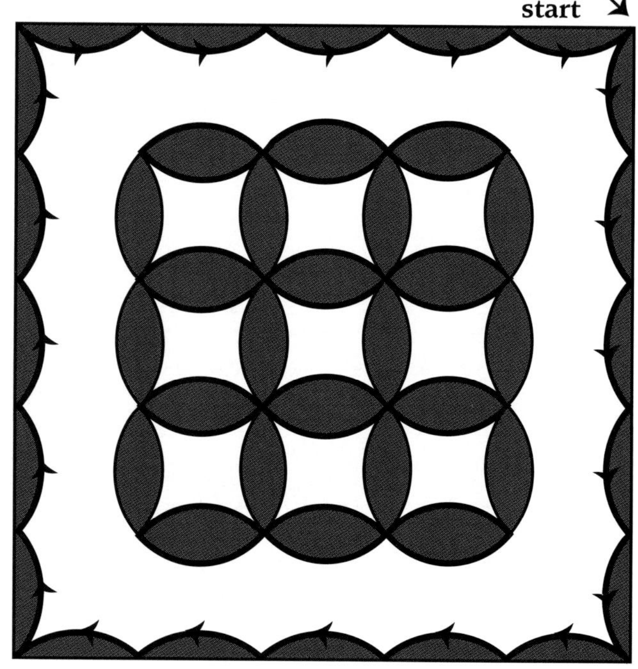

Figure 2–72. Step Four.

Appliqué the Shapes

Appliqué the top in sequence, following the diagrams above.

Finish the Quilt Top

Press the quilt top after the appliqué is done. Quilt the top. Trim off the excess fabric along the border half shapes after quilting.

Finish the Quilt

Use binding strips sewn together, end to end, with diagonal seams to bind the edges. See Closing the Circle, page 81, for finishing ideas.

Simply Circles II

By the author, 42" x 48"

Fabric & Supplies

- 1⅔ yards for the shapes, all one fabric or assorted. If using assorted fabrics, allow 3" x 6½" for each whole shape and 2" x 6½" for each half shape.
- 1⅝ yards for the background. Choose a fabric on which drawn placement lines will show.
- ½ yard for the binding
  Note: If the same fabric is used for the shapes and the binding, 2 yards will be needed.
- Batting 46" x 51"
- 3 yards of backing 46" x 51"
  (2 panels - 23" x 51")
- Fusible web 4 yards
- Machine embroidery thread
- Templates E and F for Simply Circles
- 6" x 24" placement guide
- A marker that will show on the background fabric.

Simply Circles II Project

• Tea Leaf • Compass • Lover's Knot • Lafayette Orange Peel • Circle Upon Circle • Bay Leaf • Pin Cushion • Whispering Leaves • Save a Piece • Melon Patch • Flower Petals • Tea Leaf •

Embroidery detail from Simply Circles II, by the author.

Placement Guide I

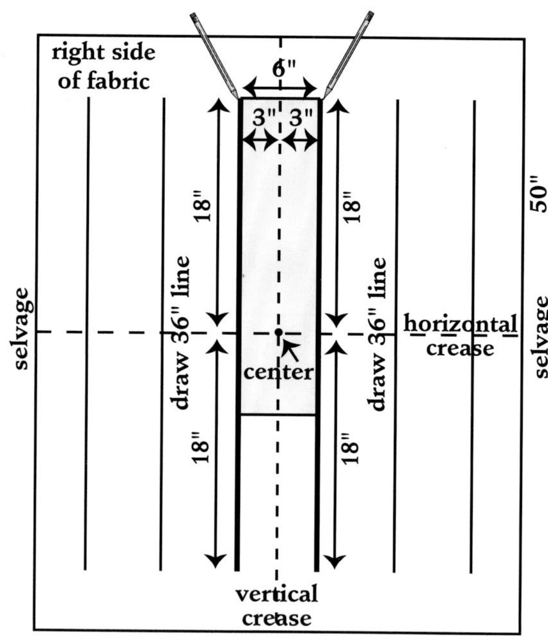

Center the ruler on the vertical crease, and mark 36" lines on either side of the ruler. Move the ruler, and continue marking vertical lines, referring to the diagram.

Prepare the Shapes

Trace Template E on the fusible web seventy-one times. Trace Template F on the fusible web thirty times. Fuse the shapes to the desired fabrics, and cut them out accurately.

Prepare the Background

1. Cut the fabric to the correct length and find the center. Do not cut off the selvages. They will be cut off later. First, press the fabric and cut the length to 50". Leave the width of the fabric as it is. In this project, the sample is 42" x 50". Each project may vary, depending on the width of the fabric. To find the center, fold the fabric right sides together with the edges lined up, and press a centered vertical crease, then refold, and press a centered horizontal crease

2. Draw lines on the right side of the fabric. When drawing the placement lines, be as accurate as possible. Use the 6" x 24" guide for all of the measuring steps and draw with a marker that will show on the fabric. There will be no lines drawn on the vertical crease. Use it as a measuring guide.

3. All vertical lines will be 36" long. Each line will extend 18" above and 18" below the horizontal crease. Center the ruler's lengthwise 3" line on the vertical crease. Mark the lines on both sides of the ruler. Using the 6" width of the ruler, continue drawing the remaining 36" lines. There will be six vertical lines. See Placement Guide I.

4. Draw a 30" line on the horizontal crease. The line will extend 15" on either side of the vertical crease. Using the 6" width of the ruler, continue drawing the remaining 30" lines, forming a grid. There will be seven 30" horizontal lines. Draw lines for the border shapes, 6" from the outside lines of the grid. Mark the border placement lines with dots every 6". See Placement Guide II.

Placement Guide II

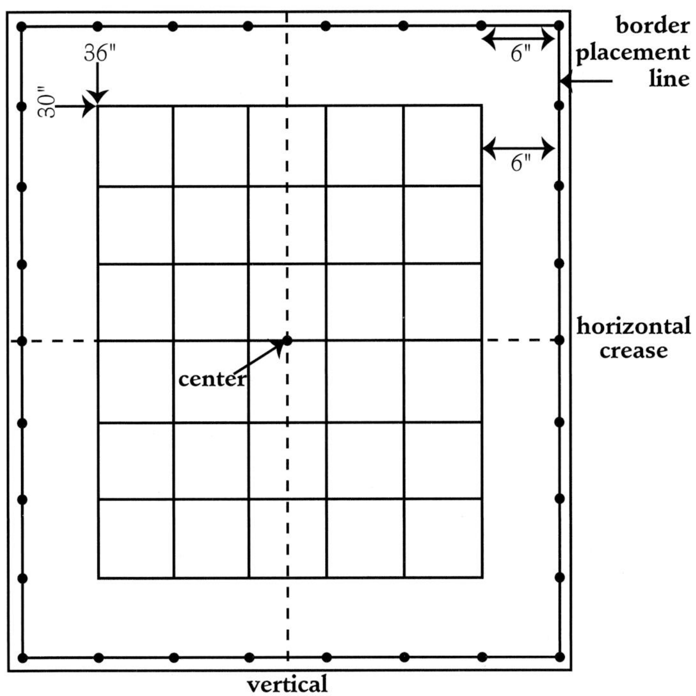

Fuse the Shapes

Fuse the shapes to the prepared background by placing and lightly fusing the shapes one row across at a time. The border half shapes go between the 6" dots and may slightly overlap. After all of the shapes are lightly fused, firmly press the top and back (Figure 2–73).

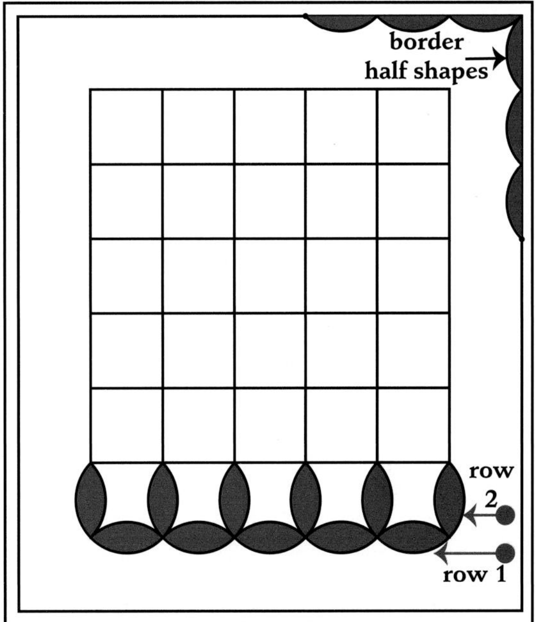

Figure 2–73. Fuse the whole shapes, moving across the grid lines in horizontal rows. Fuse the border half shapes on the outer placement line.

Kid's Stuff

For a great kid's quilt, choose a novelty fabric for the background with complementary fabric shapes. Omit the border shapes.

Note: The machine redwork embroidery designs in the sample shown here were stitched after the shapes were appliquéd to the quilt top.

All templates are on pages 98 – 101.

Appliqué Diagrams

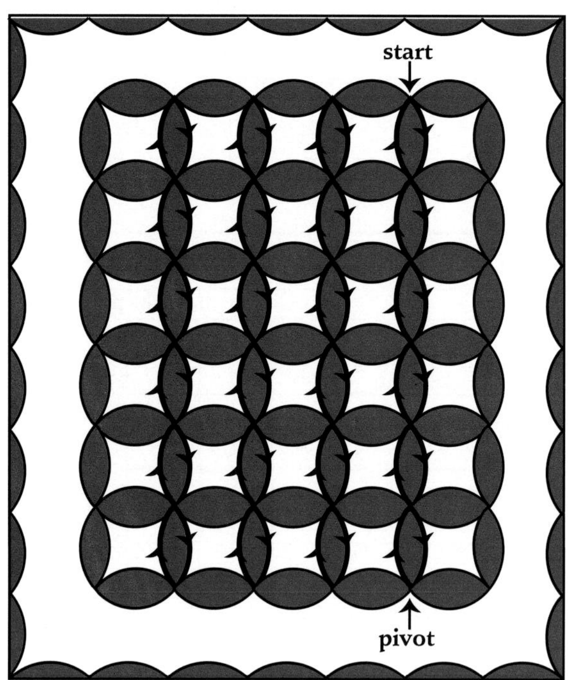

Figure 2–74. Step One.

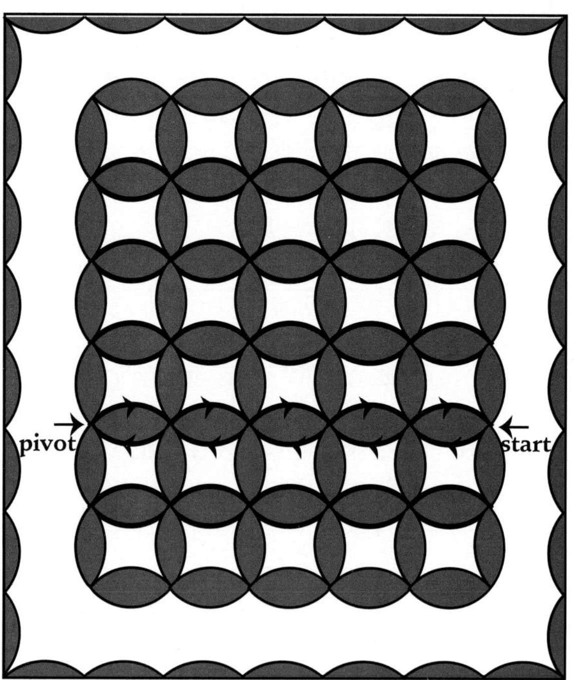

Figure 2–75. Step Two.

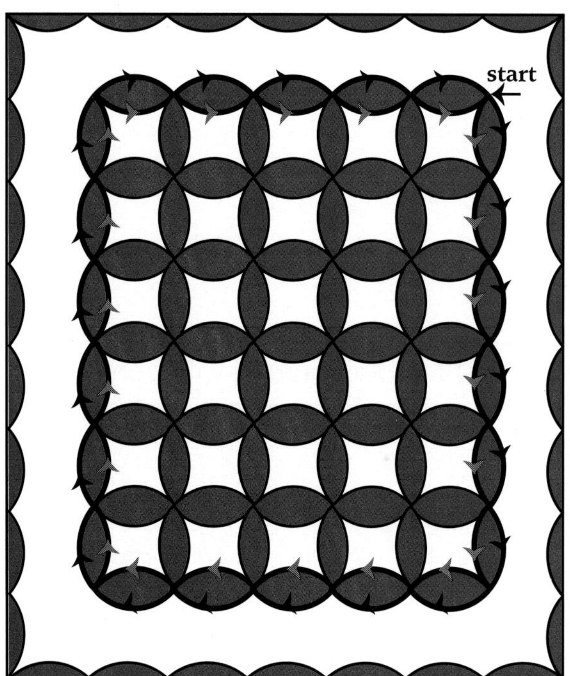

Figure 2–76. Step Three.

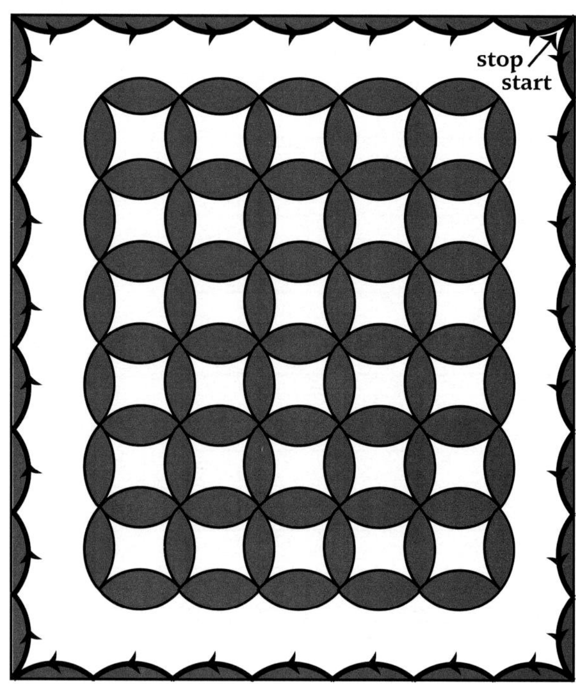

Figure 2–77. Step Four.

Appliqué the Shapes

Appliqué the top in sequence, following the diagrams.

Finish the Quilt

Press the quilt top after the appliqué is done. Quilt the top. Trim off the excess fabric along the border half shapes after quilting. To finish the edges, use your favorite techniques, or see Closing the Circle, page 81, for finishing ideas.

Simply Circles with Seamless Borders

By the author, 42" x 48"

Fabric & Supplies

- ¾ yard each of two fabrics for shapes in two colors, or 1½ yards of one fabric for shapes in only one color
- ⅝ yard each of two fabrics for the background blocks
- 1⅝ yards for the seamless borders
- ½ yard for the binding. *Note*: If the same fabric is used for the borders and the binding, 2 yards will be needed.
- Batting 46" x 51
- 3 yards of backing 46" x 51" (2 panels - 23" x 51")
- 2 yards fusible web
- Machine embroidery thread
- Template E for Simply Circles

Simply Circles with Seamless Borders Project

• Tea Leaf • Compass • Lover's Knot • Lafayette Orange Peel • Circle Upon Circle • Bay Leaf • Pin Cushion • Whispering Leaves • Save a Piece

Placement Guide

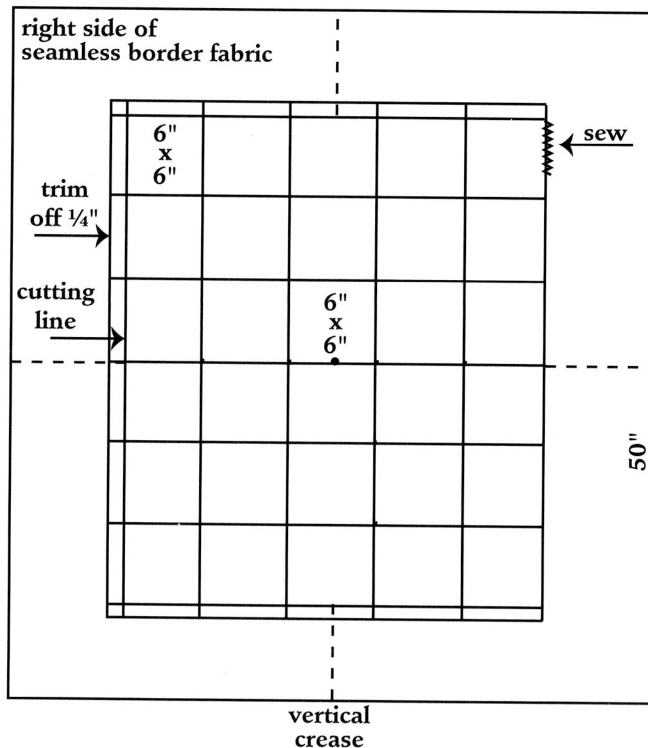

Prepare the Shapes

Trace Template E on the fusible web seventy-one times. If using two colors for the shapes, fuse 35 web shapes to one color and fuse 36 web shapes to the other color. If using only one color for the shapes, fuse all web shapes to the desired fabric. Accurately cut the shapes.

Prepare the Background

Cut fifteen 6½" x 6½" blocks from each of the background block fabrics to create the pieced background. You will have thirty blocks.

Piece the thirty background blocks in a checkerboard pattern. Press the pieced background then trim off ¼" around all four sides. See Placement Guide.

Apply Basting Strips

On the wrong side of the pieced background blocks, fuse ½" fusible web basting strips to the outside edges (Figure 2–78). Refer page 85, Preparing the Basting Strips.

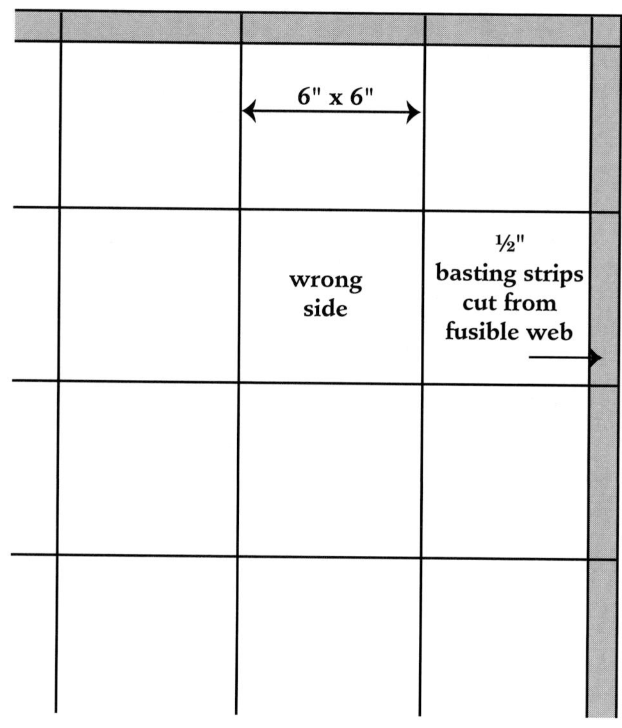

Figure 2–78. Apply ½" basting strips made of fusible web to the outside edges of the pieced background on the wrong side of the quilt top.

Appliqué Diagrams

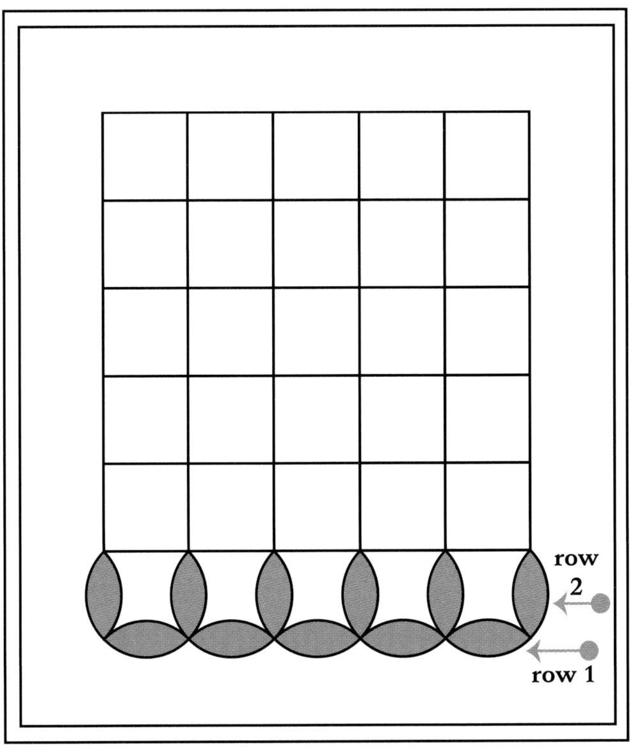

Figure 2–79. Fuse the shapes on the pieced block seams, moving across the background in horizontal rows.

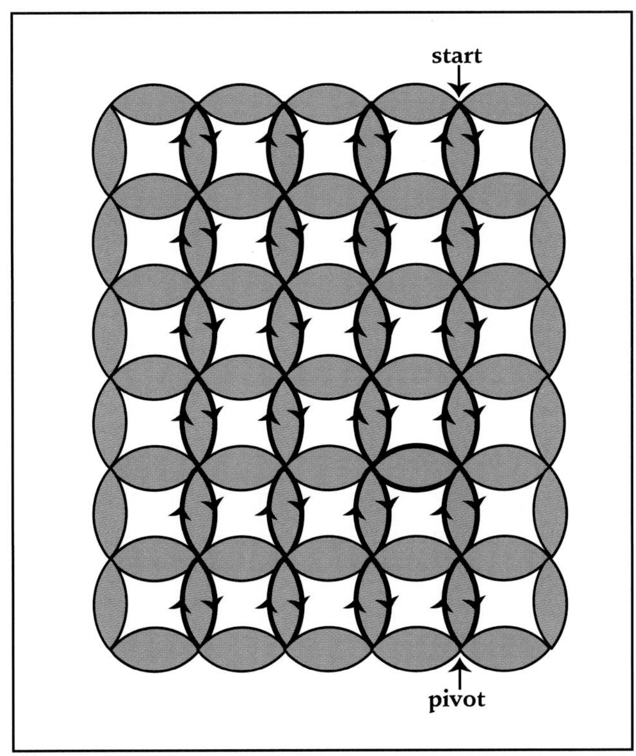

Figure 2–80. Step One.

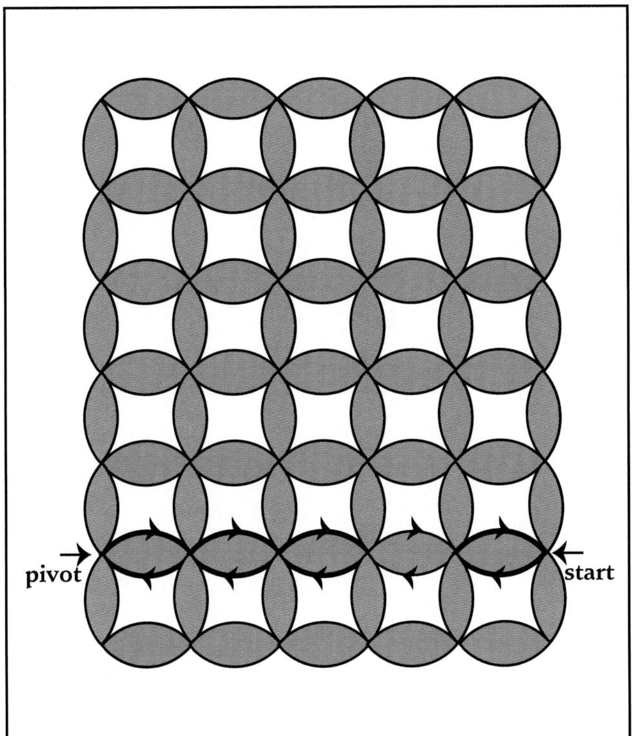

Figure 2–81. Step Two.

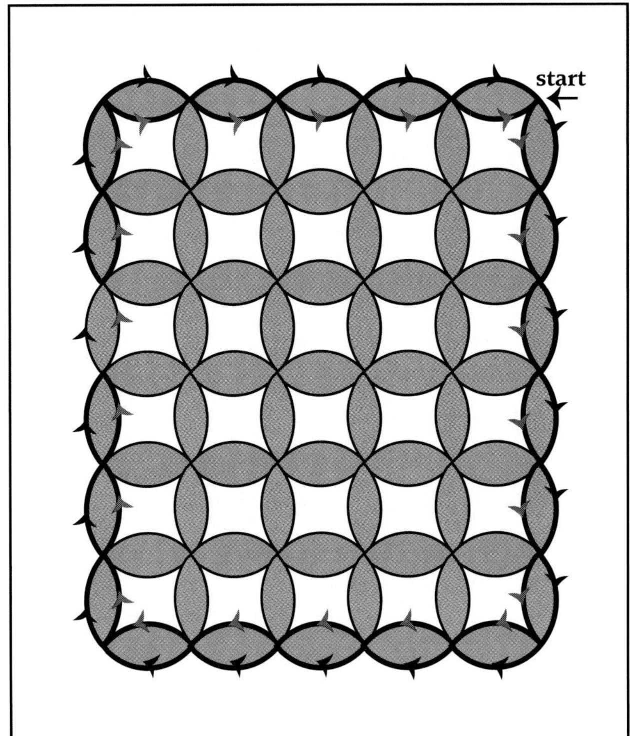

Figure 2–82. Step Three.

Prepare the Seamless Border

1. Do *not* cut off the selvages. They will be cut off later.

2. Cut the border fabric to 50" long. Leave the width of the fabric as it is. In this project, the sample is 42" x 50". Each project may vary, depending on the width of the fabric. To find the center, fold the fabric, right sides together with the edges lined up, and press a center vertical crease, then refold, and press a center horizontal crease. Refer to Placement Guide, page 72.

3. Center the pieced blocks on the *right* side of the seamless border fabric, aligning the pieced blocks with the crease lines. Fuse the pieced blocks in place. With a fine thread and a zigzag stitch, sew the blocks to the border around the edges. Refer to Placement Guide.

Fuse the Shapes

Fuse the shapes to the pieced background by placing and lightly fusing the shapes one row across at a time, over the block seams. After all of the shapes are lightly fused, firmly press the top and the back (refer to Figure 2-79 on page 73). Carefully cut away the border fabric from *behind* the pieced blocks along the zigzag stitching.

Appliqué the Shapes

Appliqué the top in sequence, following the appliqué diagrams on page 73. (Figure 2-79 through 2-82).

Finish the Quilt Top

Press the quilt top and square the quilt top an equal distance from the appliquéd shapes. Find the narrowest distance, and use that measurement to trim all four sides.

Finish the Quilt

Cut five 2½" strips to make binding. Use your favorite techniques, or see Closing the Circle, page 80, for finishing ideas.

Mysterious Circles variation
by Pennie Horras

EDGING THE CIRCLE

Curved Borders

Curved borders start with extra-wide straight borders. All that is needed to create the border curves are curved shapes. Sometimes I gather up objects with curved edges, such as salad and dinner plates, platters, and so on, from around the house, place them on the border, and see how the curves match up with the quilt. As long as the border widths on a quilt top are wide enough to accommodate a curved shape, you do not have to decide to curve the borders until after the quilting is done.

The curved border for the Mysterious Circles project in Chapter Two was created with a 16" pizza pan. The border for that project will be used here to describe the process.

Prepare the Border

• Mark the border curves on the right and wrong sides of the quilt top before basting the three layers. Use a marker that shows on the fabric and a 16" pizza pan or circle. Begin by placing the pan with one edge centered on the second block from the border seam. Measure from the border seam to the outside edge of the pizza pan. The measurement should be about 4" (Figure 3-1). Set the pan aside.

• Draw a line parallel to the seam on the border all the way around, 4" from the border seam. Draw the line on the right side and the wrong side of the quilt top (Figure 3-1).

• Place the pizza pan over the circles, matching the pan and the circles the best you can. The circles on the quilt will be slightly smaller than the pan. Align the edge of the pan with the drawn line on the border, and trace the curves on the border. Slightly overlap the marks where the curves meet. Do this on both sides (Figure 3-2).

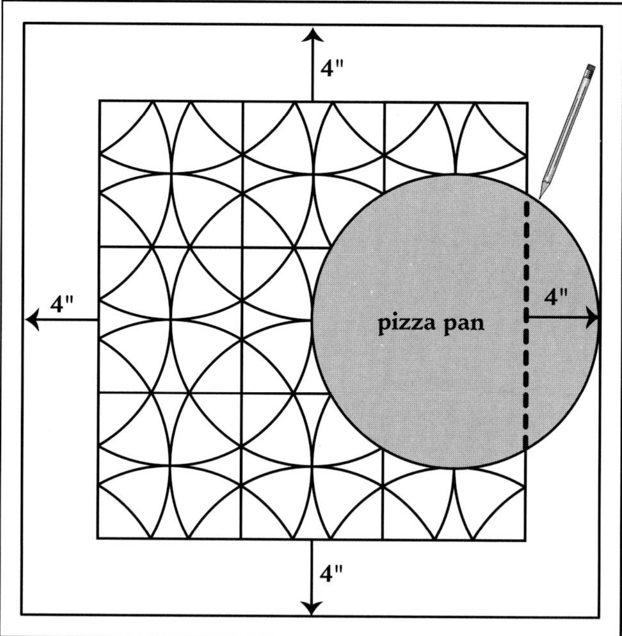

Figure 3–1. Place a pizza pan with one edge centered on the second block from the border seam. Measure the distance from the border seam to the edge of the pizza pan. Measure 4" out from the border seam and draw a line parallel with the border seam. Draw on the right and wrong sides.

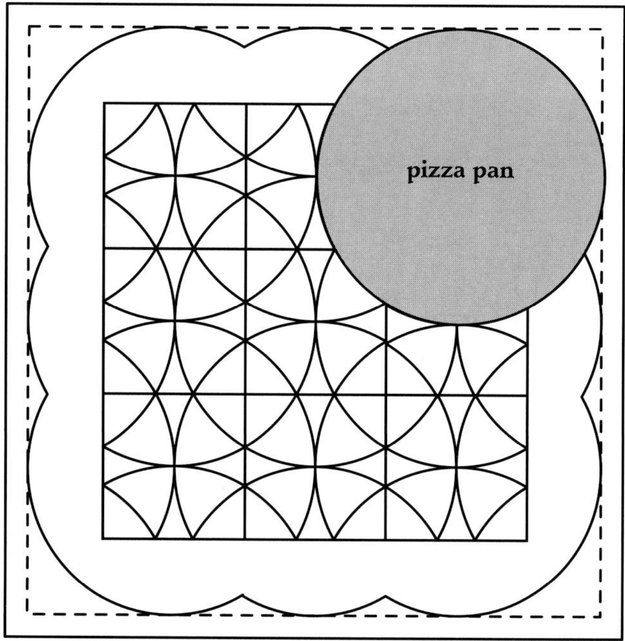

Figure 3–2. Place the pizza pan on the circles of the quilt top, and trace around the edge of the pan. Slightly overlap the marks where the curves meet. Do this on both sides.

Fusible-strip Basting

To keep the curved edges from stretching, use the following fusible-strip method of basting. Using ½" strips of fusible web, start anywhere on the marked curve on the *wrong* side of the quilt top, and fuse the strips over the marked curved line. The strips are not flexible, so bend, pleat, and fuse the best you can. Continue fusing the strips in diagonal lines over the entire quilt back about 3" to 4" inches apart (Figure 3–3).

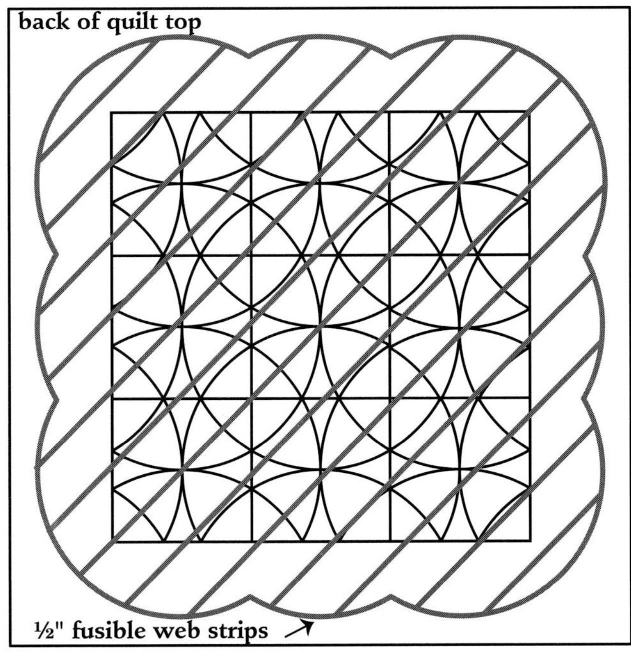

Figure 3–3. On the wrong side of the quilt top, fuse ½" basting strips of fusible web on the border curves and across the entire back.

Baste the layers and quilt the top, referring to Closing the Circle, page 80. Be sure not to quilt beyond the marked curve.

Press the quilt. To keep the curves from shifting, be sure all layers around the marked curves are securely fused.

With a thread color you can see on the fabric, sew a scant ¼" zigzag stitch centered right over the curved line. Notice where the circle lines criss-cross, round these off while sewing (Figure 3–4).

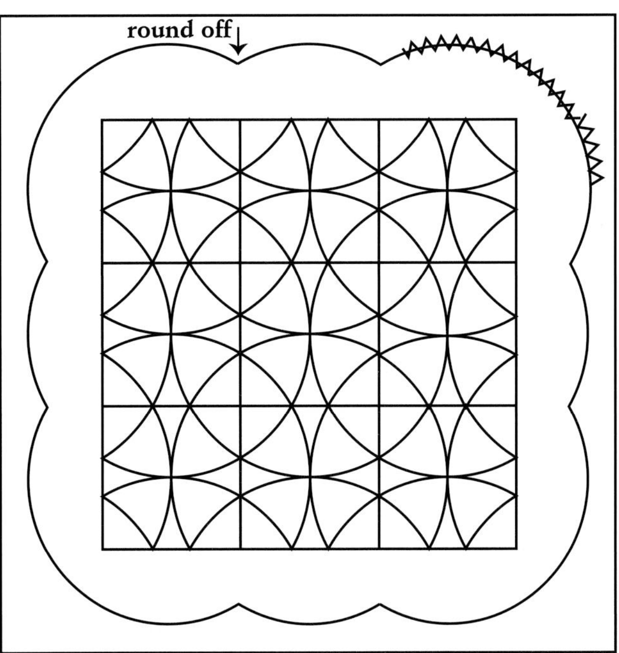

Figure 3–4. Sew a narrow zigzag stitch over the curved line on the border. Round off the curves where the lines criss-cross.

Bias Binding

Use your favorite technique, or see Closing the Circle, page 80.

There are two different methods I use to attach the bias binding with fusible web.

Method 1: Cut away the excess fabric next to the zigzag stitching and then attach the binding. Use the same attaching methods as straight binding, except there are no corners. With the raw edges of the binding and quilt top lined up, start applying the binding slightly off the center of a curve. Do not stretch while fusing. The folded edge of the binding will curl up a little while you are fusing and sewing. That's okay. The folded edge will fold nicely to the back.

Method 2: Fuse and sew the binding to the quilt by following the zigzag stitches, then cut off the excess.

Borders for Curves, Any Size

1. Borders must be cut wide enough to accommodate the curves. If you use another size of curved object to draft a pattern, use the same object for measuring. The 16" pizza pan is used here for demonstration.

2. Lay the quilt top, minus the borders, on a cutting mat. Align the edge of the quilt with one of the ruled mat lines.

3. Position the curved object with one edge centered on the second block from the quilt edge. The object should be centered over an appliquéd shape.

4. Measure from the quilt edge to the edge of the curved object and add 1½" (Figure 3–5).

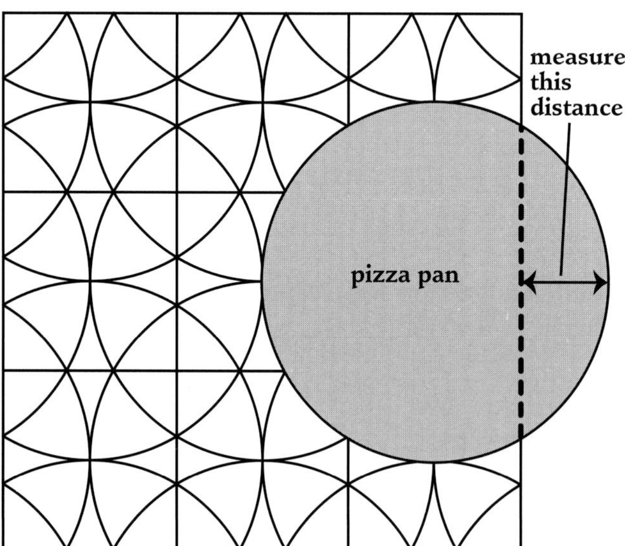

Figure 3–5. Place the curved object with one edge centered on the second block from the border seam, centered over an appliquéd shape. Measure the distance from the quilt edge to the edge of the curved object and add 1½".

5. Cut the borders to the appropriate width. In the pizza pan example, the distance from the edge of the quilt to the edge of the pan measured 4". The borders would be cut 5½" wide.

Piping

Piping can be inserted in any seam. The most common application is in conjunction with the binding or between the borders and quilt seams. It's a great enhancing accessory.

Piping is added just before the binding to straight or curved-edge quilts and can be any width desired. Fabric strips 1" wide finish about ¼" wide. This is the size used here to describe the process.

Piping for Straight Edges

1. Measure the length of each side of the quilt and add 1". Cut four piping fabric strips 1" wide by the measured length.

2. Lay the piping strips wrong side up on an ironing surface and fuse ¼" strips of fusible web to the top edges (Figure 3–6).

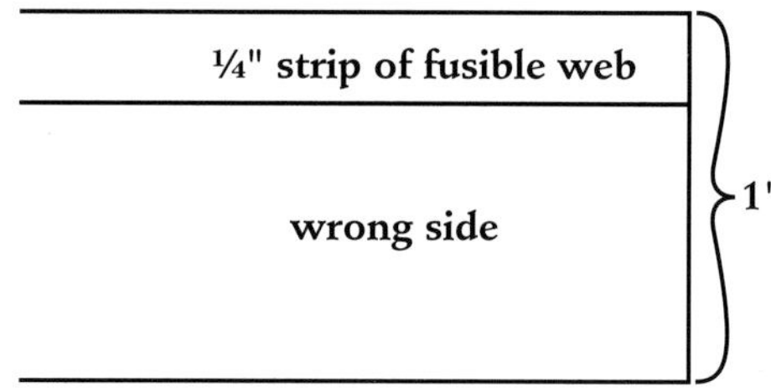

Figure 3–6 Fuse ¼" strips of fusible web along the top edges of the piping strips on the wrong side of the fabric.

3. Fold each strip in half, wrong sides together, and fuse closed. Fuse another ¼" strip of fusible web along the top raw edge of each strip (Figure 3–7).

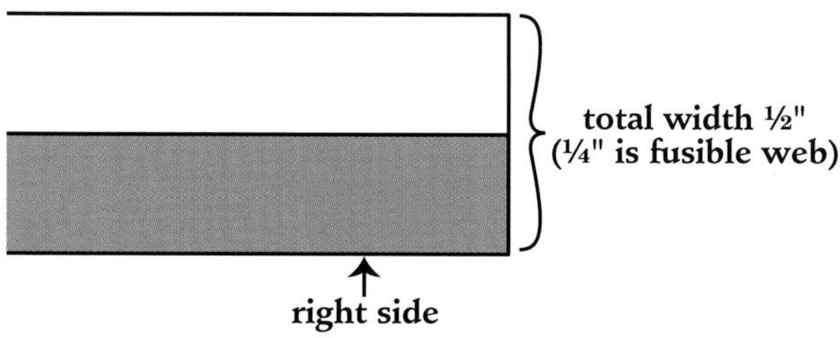

Figure 3–7. Fold each strip in half, wrong sides together and fuse closed. Fuse another ¼" strip of fusible web to the raw edges.

4. Align the raw edges of one piping strip with one raw edge of the quilt top. Center the strip so the piping extends about ½" beyond the corners. Fuse. Do the opposite side next. Then do the other two sides (Figure 3–8).

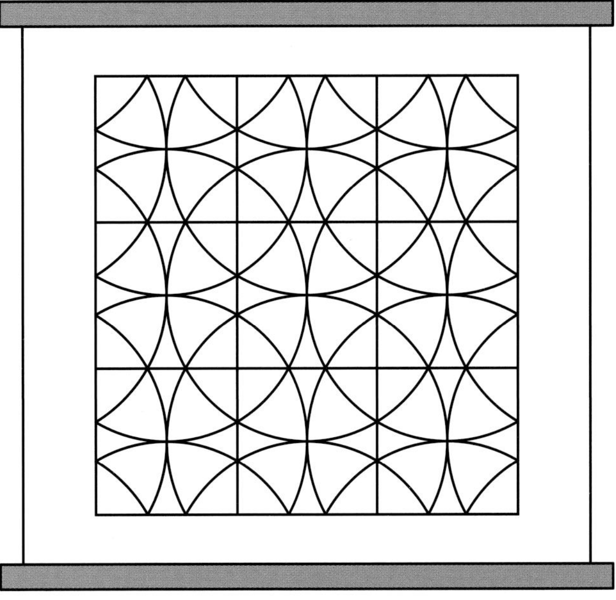

raw edge

Figure 3–8. Center one piping strip on one raw edge of the quilt top. Fuse in place. Repeat for the other sides.

Turn the quilt to the back and trim the excess piping even with the corners (Figure 3–9). Attach the binding, and finish the quilt.

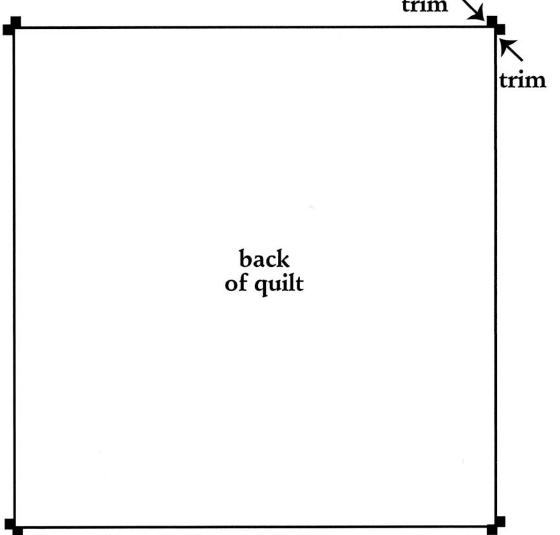

Figure 3–9. Turn the quilt over. Trim the excess piping even with the corners.

Piping for Curved Edges

Refer to double-fold bias binding or piping instructions in Closing the Circle, on page 81.

Simply Circles variation
by Sharon Brown

CLOSING THE CIRCLE

The way a quilt is finished can make the difference between an ordinary quilt and an extraordinary one. Following are my favorite methods of basting, machine quilting, squaring up, binding, and adding a sleeve. As always, experiment to find what works best for you and for each particular quilt.

Basting with Fusibles

Once upon a time, I had an outrageous collection of unfinished quilts. I finished many the usual way, but no matter how carefully I basted with safety pins or thread, I still didn't like the way they handled during quilting. Frequently, the results were unsatisfactory. I explored other possibilities and, after years of experimenting, came up with a pin-less, painless, hassle-free basting method, using fusible batting and strips of fusible web.

Quilts basted in this way will support any type of machine or hand quilting. No more struggling with shifty, creepy fabric, pleats, or wrinkles. The quilt lies flat, is easy to maneuver, and behaves admirably. This method works well with many types of batting and is washable, too.

Preparing the Basting Strips

Fusible web in ¼" and ½" strips can be purchased or can be cut from paper-backed fusible web (Refer to Starting the Circle page 8). If cutting the strips, check that the web is well attached to the paper.

Cut a supply of strips in ¼" and ½" widths. The length of the strips can vary up to 36". To cut strips, lightly fold (do not crease) the fusible web, paper side out, in half once or twice. Lay a ruler on the left end of the folded web. The ruler helps hold the web in place during cutting. From the right side, slide another ruler across the folded web, and by eye or using the lines on the mat, cut the strips.

Method One: Single-sided Fusible Batting

This method uses strips of fusible web and fusible fleece, a thin batting that is fusible on one side. Following the steps carefully will ensure that the iron will not come in contact with the fusible web.

Lay the fleece on a flat surface, lay the quilt top on the fleece, and cut the fleece 1" larger than the top. Then, lay the fleece on the backing and cut the backing 1" larger than the fleece (Figure 4-1).

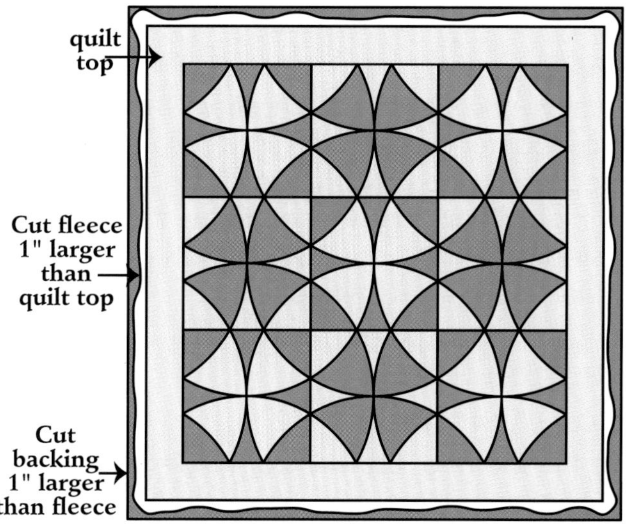

Figure 4-1. Cut the fleece 1" larger than the quilt top. Cut the backing fabric 1" larger than the fleece.

Place the fleece on an ironing surface with the fusible side up. Smooth the backing fabric wrong side down on the fleece. Using a medium hot steam iron, start fusing in the middle by lightly gliding the iron across the fabric, then fuse the entire back. It fuses quickly. Experiment with your iron.

Fuse ½" basting strips to the wrong side of the quilt top. Start in a corner and fuse the strips around all of the edges. Slightly overlap the strips. Fuse the strips one at a time in diagonal lines over the entire quilt back, about 3" to 4" apart. This is just like thread basting, except it is needed in only one direction (Figure 4-2).

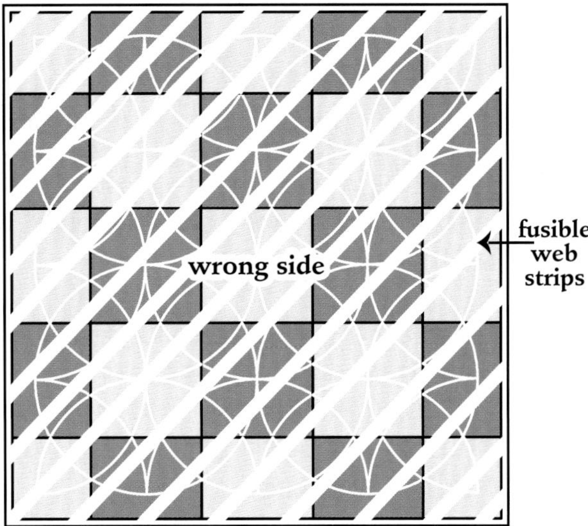

Figure 4–2. Fuse basting strips, to the wrong side of the quilt top around all edges and across the back.

Remove the paper backing from the basting strips. Center the quilt top, right side up, on the fleece and smooth it out. Starting in the center of the quilt top, fuse the top to the fleece with a steam iron. Do not fuse to the edges until after the quilting is finished.

Method Two: Non-fusible Batting

For this method, use strips of fusible web and non-fusible batting.

Fuse the basting strips to the wrong side of the backing fabric, following the same process as in Method One. This works equally well with cotton and cotton blends.

Method Three: Double-sided Fusible Batting

For this method, use batting that is fusible on both sides. The three layers are fused all at the same time. Before using the double-sided batting, read the manufacturer's instructions. Unroll the batting and let it rest for a while.

Cut the batting and the backing as in Method One, on the previous page.

Lay the pressed backing, wrong side up, on a firm ironing surface so the backing lies smoothly. Center and smooth the batting on the backing. Center and smooth the quilt top, right side up, on the batting.

Fuse the layers together with a steam iron. Start in the center of the quilt top and fuse outward toward the edges. Lift the iron up and down while fusing, being careful not to shift the three layers out of position. After the entire top is fused, turn the quilt top over and press the back. This will ensure that the back is thoroughly fused.

Hint: If there are any creases or folds on the back after the top is fused, peel up the backing fabric, smooth out the wrinkles, and thoroughly re-fuse.

Quilting by Machine

Quilt around all of the shapes as they were appliquéd or around just a few. Depending on the decorative stitch style, quilt right through the shape middles or next to the stitches. Free motion quilting in the open spaces adds texture (Figure 4–3).

Figure 4–3. Quilting adds texture and detail. Quilting can be done in the ditch, around the shapes, through the shapes or a combination of all of these.

On the borders that are going to be curved, be sure to mark the curves before quilting.

On larger quilts, do the quilting in rows from top to bottom. If the quilt has blocks, quilt the block seams in the ditch first, then quilt around the shapes. Sometimes quilting in all of the ditch seams is enough.

If the quilt is handled extensively while machine quilting, the fuse may release in places. Re-press and re-fuse as needed. When I machine quilt a large quilt, I press each row just before quilting.

If the machine embroidery and the quilting are done in one step, I frequently do additional quilting on other areas of the quilt.

Squaring Up the Quilt

After the quilting is finished, press the quilt. To prevent the edges from shifting, be sure all three layers are securely fused.

If the quilt is not straight, find something on the quilt, like a block, border seam, or design, and line up the ruler with the straightest line. Measure from this and trim edges.

Lay the quilt on a cutting mat and line up a long ruler along one edge of the quilt. Starting at the bottom, trim away the excess batting and fabric, and clean up the quilt edge. Trim all four sides before squaring the corners.

To square the corners, lay a large square ruler on a corner even with the two straight outside edges and trim any remaining excess fabric. Square all four corners.

Professional Binding

This method utilizes 1/4" strips of fusible web to baste the binding in place. It is helpful to have a supply of basting strips cut before you begin.

Double-fold Straight Grain Binding

The estimated binding length needed is given with each project.

To calculate the length needed to make double-fold straight grain binding with a finished width of 1/4", add up the number of inches around the quilt and add 10" for making corner turns and for finishing the ends. Be sure to allow enough length to include the seams between strips (2½" per seam), which are sewn on the bias.

For other binding widths, start by increasing or decreasing the strip widths in increments of 1/4" and test until you arrive at the desired finished size.

To make the binding:
Cut the binding strips 2½" wide.

Sew strips together. Lay the end of one strip across the end of another strip at right angles, right sides together, and sew the strips on the diagonal (Figure 4–4).

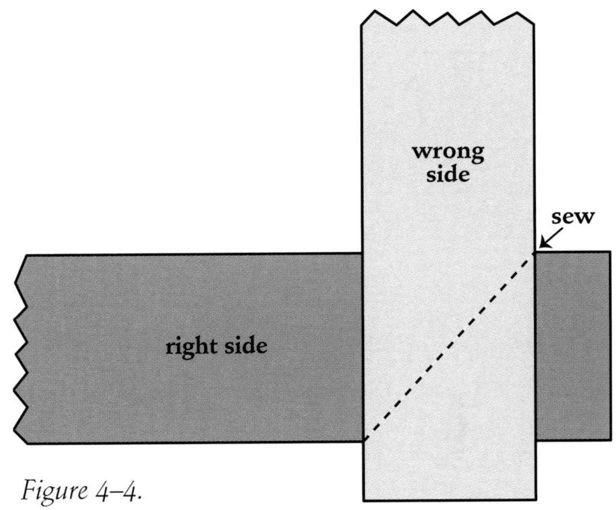

Figure 4–4.

Trim the seam allowances to 1/4" (Figure 4–5).

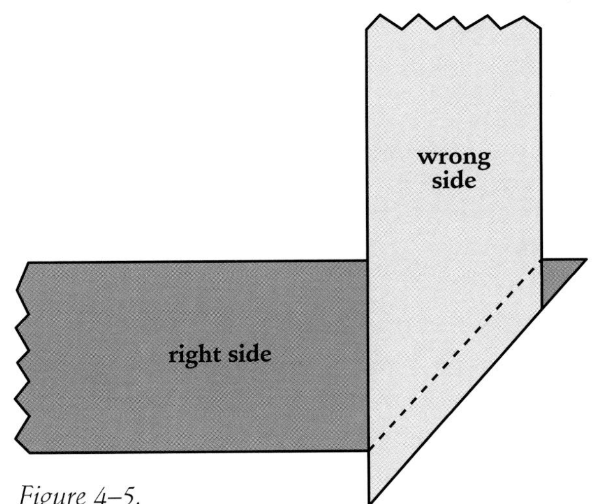

Figure 4–5.

Press the seam allowances open and trim off the little tips (Figure 4-6).

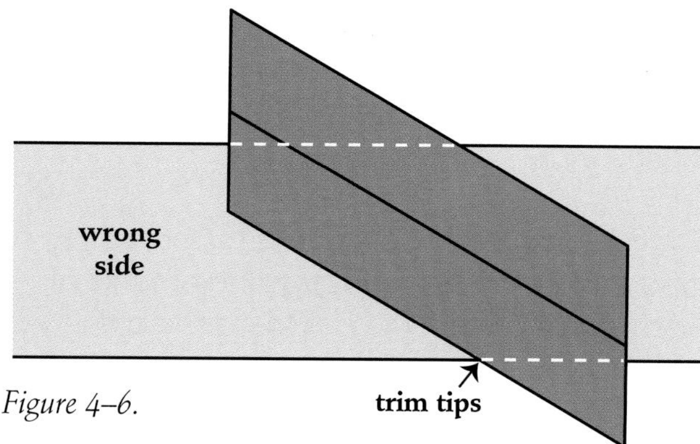

Figure 4–6.

Note: It's important that the next steps be followed as shown or all will end up backwards. Each step starts at the right end of the binding. On an ironing surface, lay the binding wrong side up facing you, with the bulk of the binding to your left. Cut a 45° angle on the right end (Figure 4-7).

Figure 4–7.

Fuse a ¼" strip of fusible web at the edge of the angled right end, peel off the backing paper, fold the end over and fuse a ¼" hem. Fuse another ¼" basting strip right over the top of the hemmed right end. Do not peel off the paper backing on hemmed edge (Figure 4-8).

Figure 4–8.

Start at the hemmed right end and fuse ¼" strips of fusible web to the top edge of the binding all the way to the opposite end. If the ends of the basting strips are overlapped when they are connected, the paper will peel off in one piece (Figure 4-9).

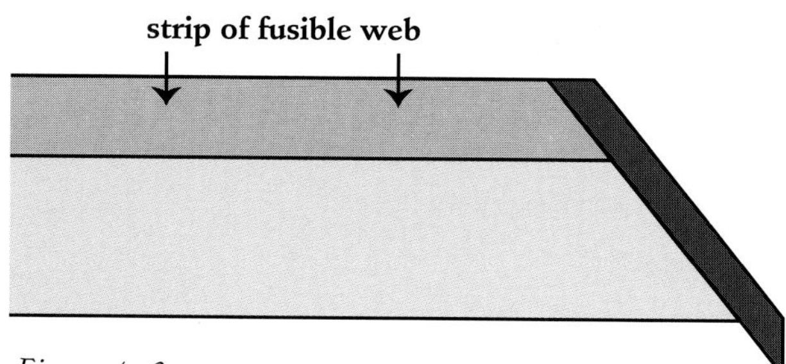

Figure 4–9.

Remove the long backing paper from the fusible web strips. Fold the binding strip, wrong sides together, and fuse the bottom edge to the top. Referring to the illustration, notice the direction of the angled end. Trim off the little tip (Figure 4-10).

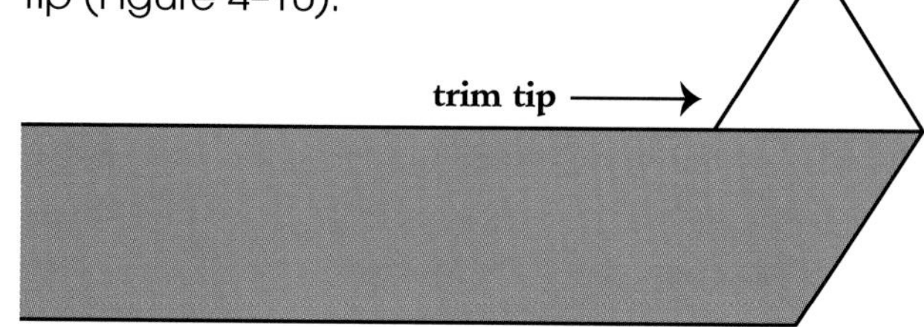

Figure 4–10.

Starting at the right end again, fuse another ¼" basting strip to the top raw edge of the binding to the opposite end (Figure 4-11).

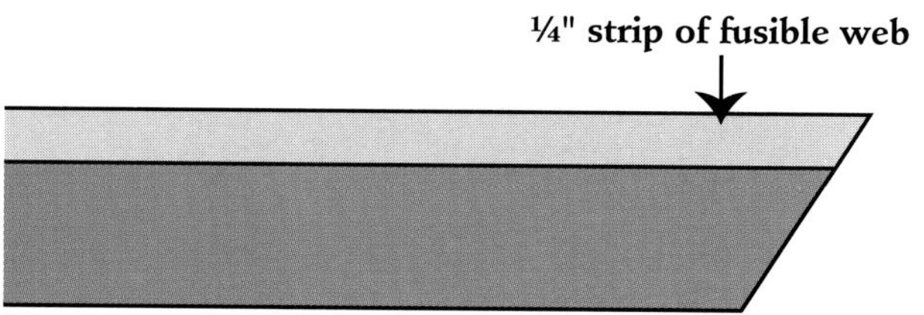

Figure 4–11.

The professional binding is now ready to attach to the quilt.

Double-fold Bias Binding or Piping

Find the length by measuring the perimeter of the quilt top For the binding, add 2½" for each connecting bias seam. For the piping, add 1" for each connecting bias seam. For both, add 10" for insurance.

To make the binding:

Prepare the fabric for the bias strips by folding it at a 45° angle with two edges lined up. Press a crease in the fold (Figure 4–12).

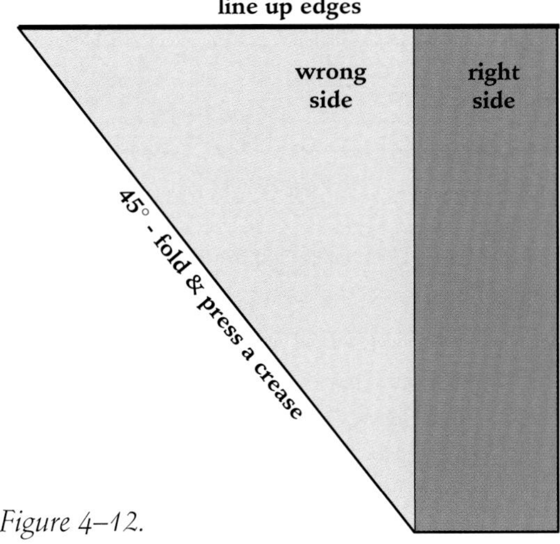

Figure 4–12.

Slice off the pressed crease and cut the 45° bias strips (Figure 4–13).

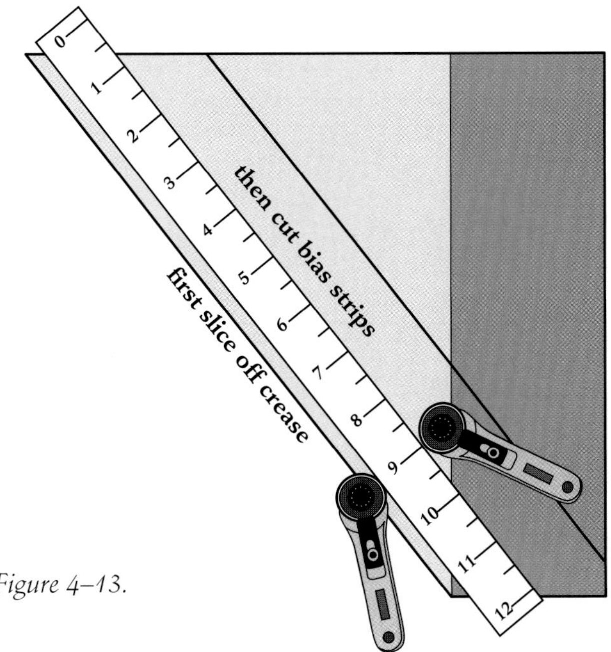

Figure 4–13.

Refer to Figure 4-4, page 83, and follow the same techniques as shown for double-fold straight grain binding.

Note: Bias piping is fused to the edges before the bias binding is attached.

Attaching the Binding

Lay the quilt, right side up with one edge facing you, on an ironing surface.

To avoid extra bulk at the corners, place the hemmed right end of the binding at approximately the center of a quilt edge and loosely arrange the binding around the quilt's perimeter. Check that the binding seams do not fall on any of the corners. If they do, adjust the binding at the beginning.

That little piece of fusible web paper backing should still be on the hemmed right end.

Remove the strip of backing paper and place the hemmed right end of the binding at the beginning point on the quilt edge. With all the raw edges even, fuse the binding to the quilt edge. Stop at the first corner (Figure 4–14).

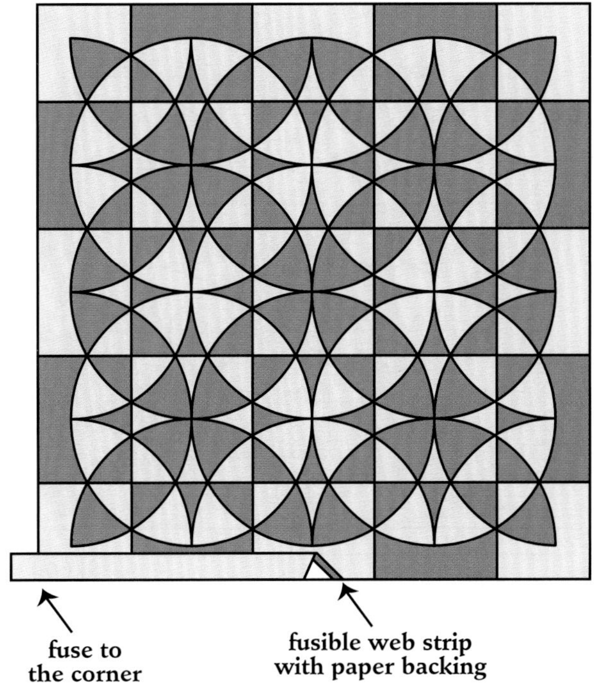

Figure 4–14.

Rotate the quilt one-quarter turn. At the corner, fold the binding away from the quilt at right angles, forming a miter. Press and crease the miter (Figure 4–15).

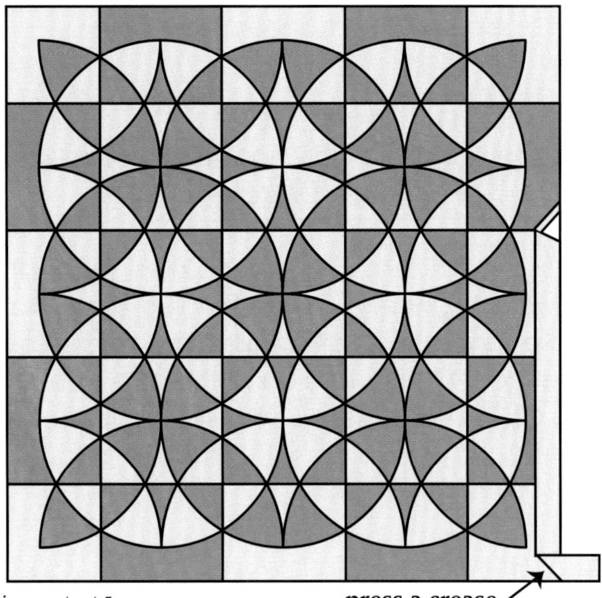

Figure 4–15.

Fold the binding down over itself, forming a fold that is even with or just a scant bit below the raw edge of the quilt. Press the fold, line up the binding with the next edge and continue fusing the binding to the quilt (Figure 4–16).

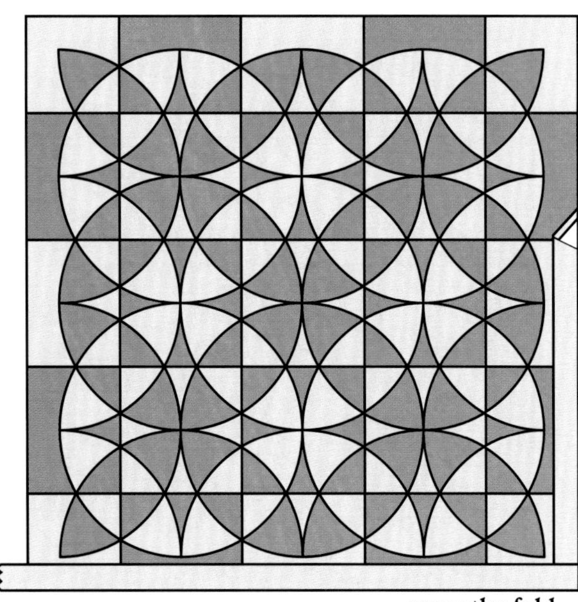

Figure 4–16.

Open up 2"-3" of the binding and peel off the small piece of backing paper. Trim the excess from the tail and slip it inside the end about 2" or 3". Line up the edges and finish fusing in place (Figure 4–17).

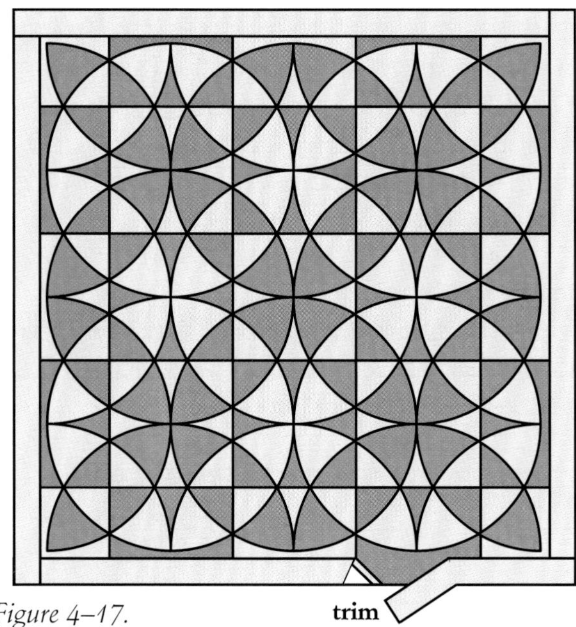

Figure 4–17.

Many quiltmakers are unhappy with their quilt's binding and mitered corners. It is probably because the seams are not sewn exactly straight along the edges and into the corners. The sewing tends to veer off a little one way or the other. Try the following method for better results.

To sew the binding in place:
Using a ¼" seam, start sewing 2" to 3" below a corner. Just before arriving at the corner, lift up the pressed fold and sew to the pressed crease. Stop sewing with the needle down in the crease. Backstitch a few stitches and remove the quilt. Reposition the quilt and sew each remaining side, in the same way (Figure 4–18).

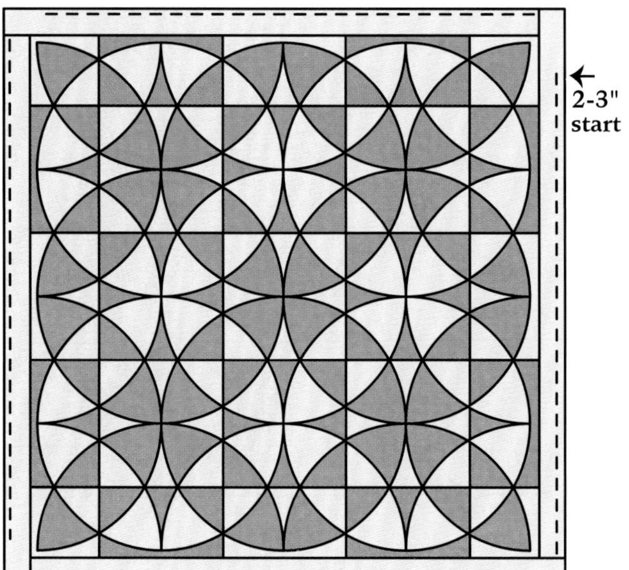

Figure 4–18.

Turn the quilt to the back side and finish sewing the remaining 2" to 3" on each side, sewing toward the corner. Overlap a few stitches at the start, and continue sewing right off the end of the quilt. Be careful not to disturb the mitered corner fold underneath. Leave it folded as it was pressed (Figure 4–19).

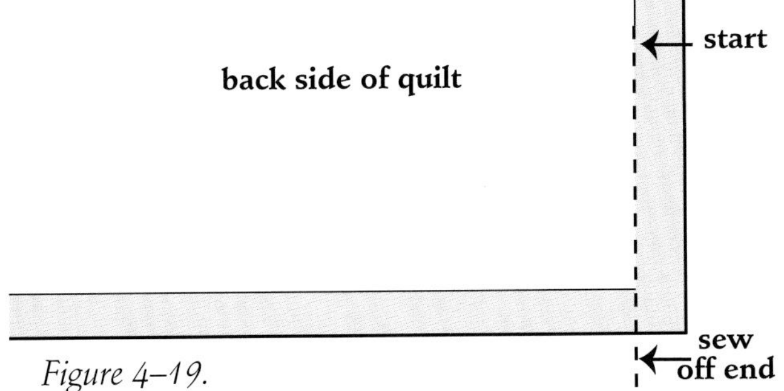

Figure 4–19.

Turn the quilt right side up and press the binding out from the top. Stop pressing ½" from each corner, so as not to distort the miters (Figure 4–20).

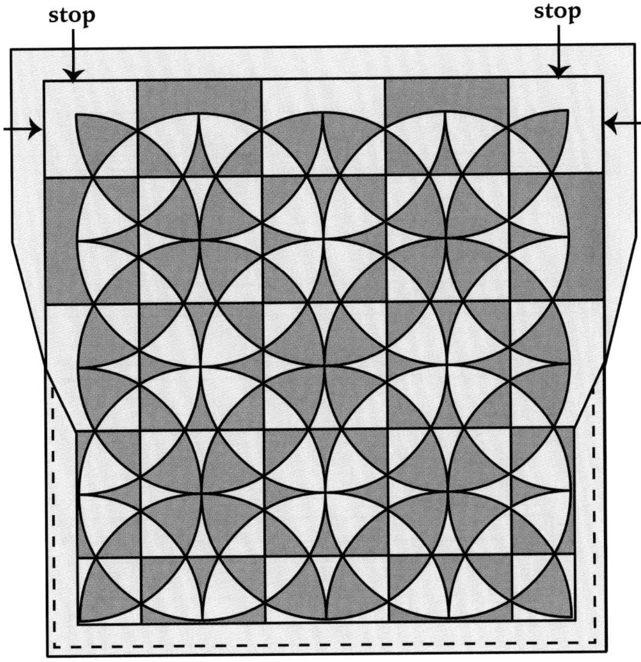

Figure 4–20.

On the back of the quilt, fuse ¼" strips of fusible web just above the ¼" seam line on all edges. There is no need to fuse the strips completely into the corners (Figure 4–21).

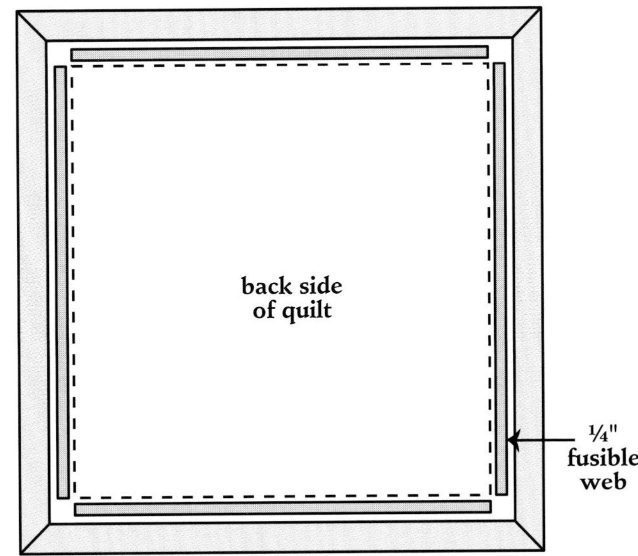

Figure 4–21.

Remove the backing paper from the ¼" strips of fusible web. Starting at the center of one side, gently fold the binding to the back (it will cover the stitches) and fuse in place. Form and press in the miters as you go along. Hand sew the binding and corners in place (Figure 4–22).

Figure 4–22.

Sleeves for Hanging Quilts

The finished width of the sleeve can very depending on the size of the quilt. When cutting fabric for the sleeve, allow at least 9" for a large quilt and no less than 6" for a small one. The construction is the same for any sized sleeve. For larger quilts, make two sleeves and leave a space in the middle for a rod bracket.

A. At the top back of the quilt, measure the length inside the binding, minus 1", and choose the desired finished width. Cut the sleeve fabric as along as the inside measurement and slightly more than twice the desired finished width. Hem the two short ends with ¼" strips of fusible web or cut the ends with pinking shears. Fold the sleeve in half, wrong sides together, and sew ¼" seam the length of the sleeve (Figure 4-23).

B. Center the seam on the sleeve and press it open. This will be the back. Then press the entire sleeve flat, so there are two creased folds, equal distance from the seam. Sew a row of stitches along one of the folds as close to the edge as possible. On the back, draw a line ½" from the opposite creased fold (Figure 4-24).

C. Press a new fold on the drawn line and sew another row of stitches along this fold (Figure 4-25).

D. Press the sleeve flat, leaving a loose fold above one line of stitches. For a quick and accurate way to place and baste the sleeve to the quilt, fuse ½" fusible strips along and just inside the two rows of stitches and at each end. Remove the backing paper from the strips (Figure 4-26).

E. On the top back of the quilt, place the loose sleeve fold just under the binding and centered on the quilt. Fuse the sleeve to the quilt. This acts as temporary basting. Hand-sew the sleeve to the quilt along the top and bottom rows of machine stitching and at the ends (Figure 4-27).

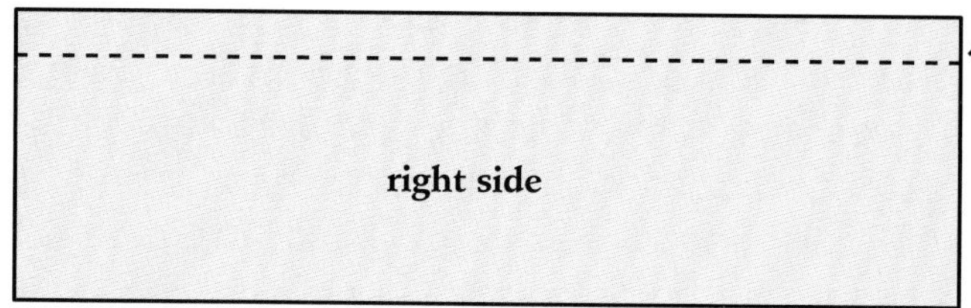

Figure 4–23.

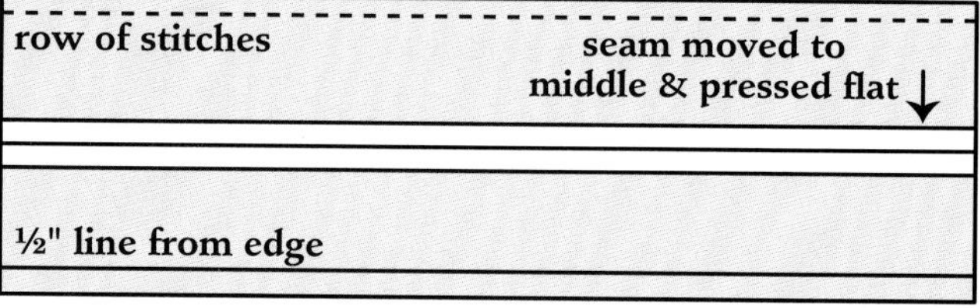

Figure 4–24.

Figure 4–25.

Figure 4–26.

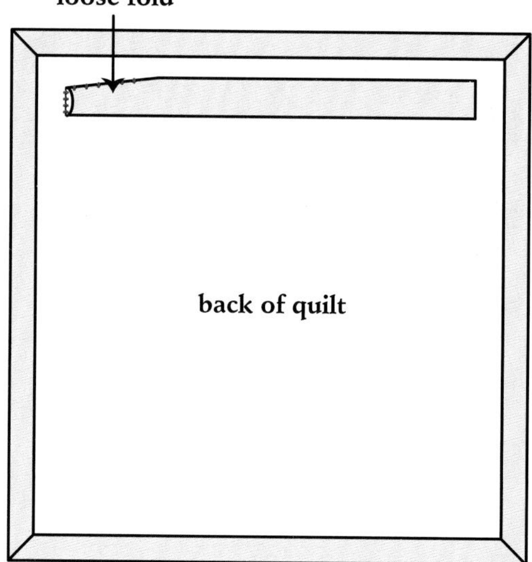

Figure 4–27.

Mysterious Ovals variation
by Mary Johnson

Extra Circular Activities Making Templates Any Size

Circle Quilt designs are versatile and can be adapted to fit any desired size. After you have drafted a few patterns yourself, you may never look at a dinner plate the same way again.

Mysterious Circles

After much use, my original template was getting a little ragged, and I didn't have a compass. My daughter-in-law noticed my large circle quilt and said, "Ah, a pizza pan quilt." Ever since then, I draft new patterns by using circular objects from around the house. In the Mysterious Circle classes I teach, the supplies and tools to bring from home include a 16" pizza pan or a comparable circular object. The first step in class is to make the template. I offer the pizza pan or the compass method. Invariably, students choose to use the pizza pan, which is much easier to control. Everything from a round roasting pan lid to a garbage can lid has been used. It makes for an interesting and fun start to a class.

Any size of circular object will work for a Mysterious Circles pattern, and the quilt block will be exactly half the size of the object. Thus, a 16" circular object will make an 8" quilt block. This is the size used to describe how to draft the pattern.

Supplies

- A circle with smooth, even edges
- Two pieces of paper you can see pencil lines through. The paper size should be at least 2" larger all around than the circular object you are using.
- Pencils
- Rulers, a long rectangle and a large square

The Pattern

Trace the circular object on one piece of the see-through paper (Figure 5-1).

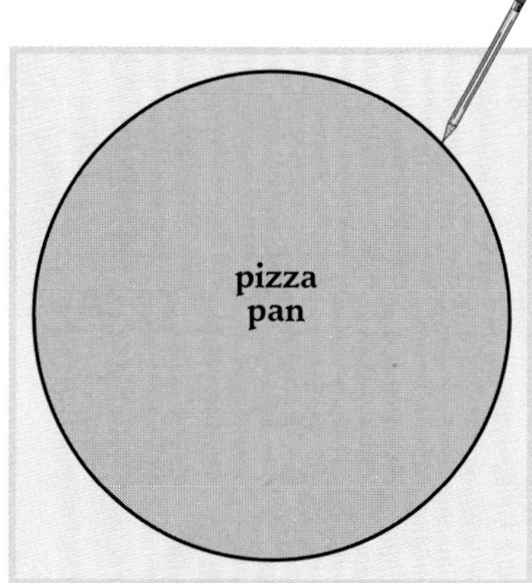

Figure 5–1. Trace the circular object.

Fold the paper in half, align the traced lines, and finger press a crease (Figure 5-2).

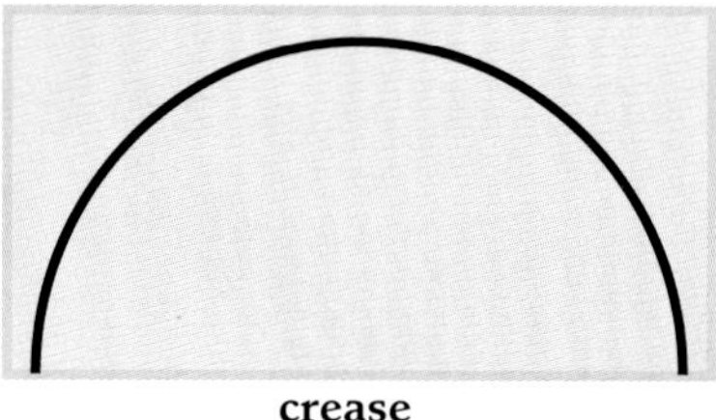

Figure 5–2. Fold the tracing paper in half and crease it.

Unfold the paper and draw a line on the crease from edge to edge of the circle. Measure the line and make a note of this measurement. This is the circle's diameter. Lay this paper aside (Figure 5-3).

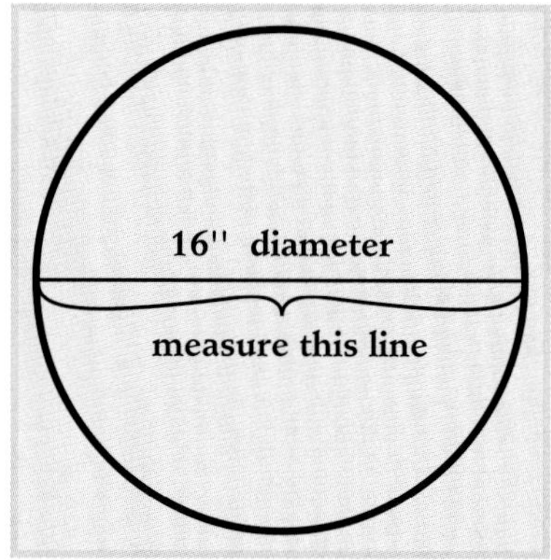

Figure 5–3. Draw a line along the crease and measure.

On the other piece of paper, draw a square the exact size of the circle diameter. Divide the square into four equal sections. To do this, fold the paper in half, align the pencil lines, and finger press a crease. Unfold the paper, and draw a line on the crease. Repeat the process, folding the paper in the other direction (Figure 5–4).

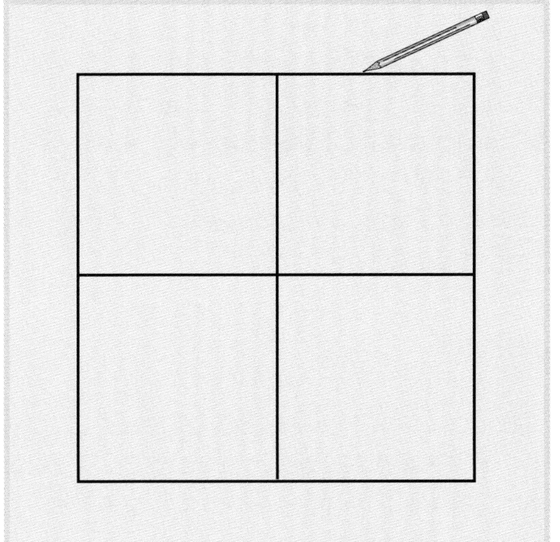

Figure 5–4. Draw a square the size of the circle's diameter. Fold the in quarters and draw lines along the folds.

Align the edge of the circular object with the center intersection of the drawn square. Trace around the circle from corner to corner. Be sure to draw over the center intersecting lines (Figure 5–5).

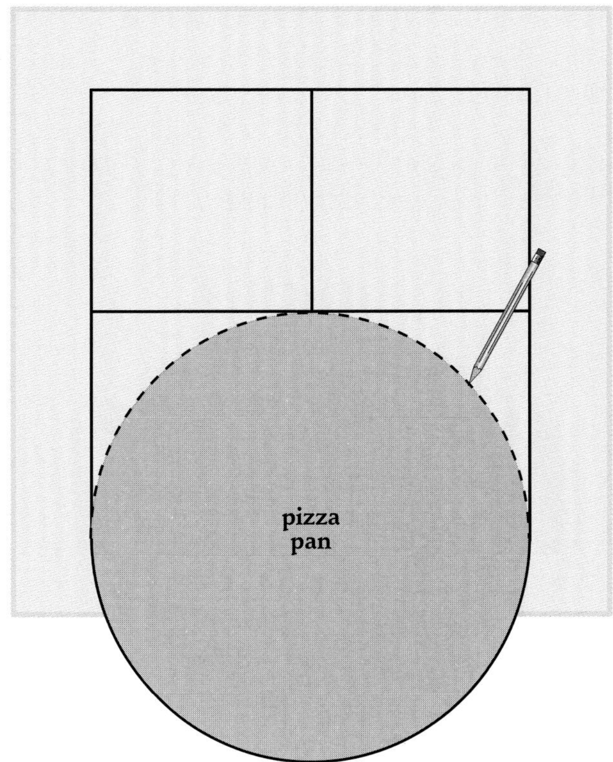

Figure 5–5. Position the circular object and trace it.

Move the circular object and trace around it on each side of the square, four times all together (Figure 5–6).

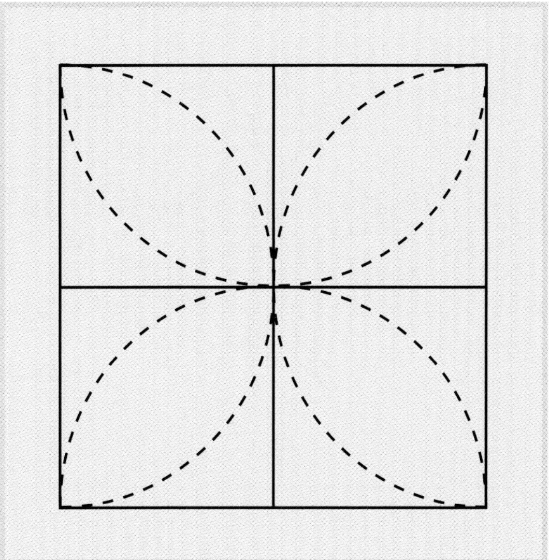

Figure 5–6. Reposition the circular object and trace around it. Repeat for each side.

Align the edges of the circular object with the straight lines in the middle of the square and trace. Repeat for every corner (Figure 5–7).

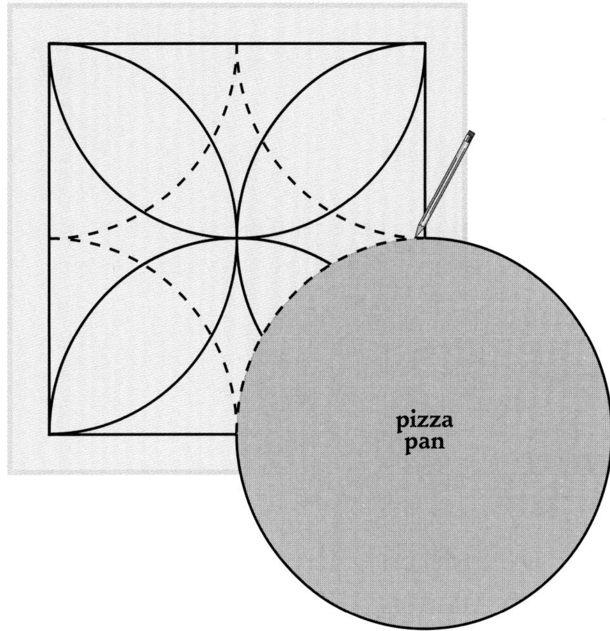

Figure 5–7. Reposition and trace in each corner.

Using a square ruler, isolate the shape in the middle, and draw a square around the shape. Be sure all tips are equally squared up. Measure the size of the square, and write this size on the paper. With a pencil, draw an arrow at each tip of the shape (Figure 5-8).

Figure 5–8. Draw a square around the central shape and mark the tips with arrows and measure the square.

Make a template of the center shape (Figure 5-9).

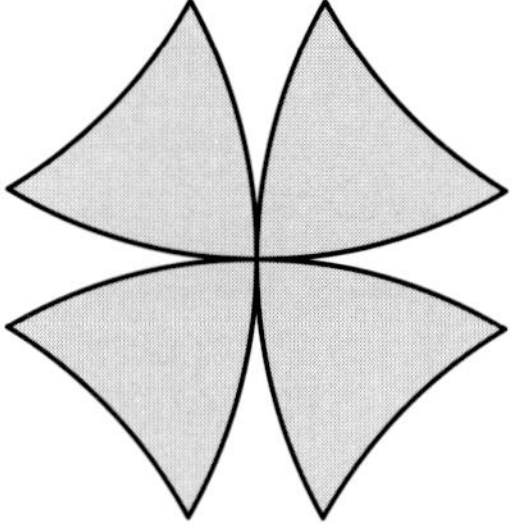

Figure 5–9. Use the center shape to make a template.

The placement guide is the size of the center square. Transfer the arrows to the placement guide (Figure 5-10).

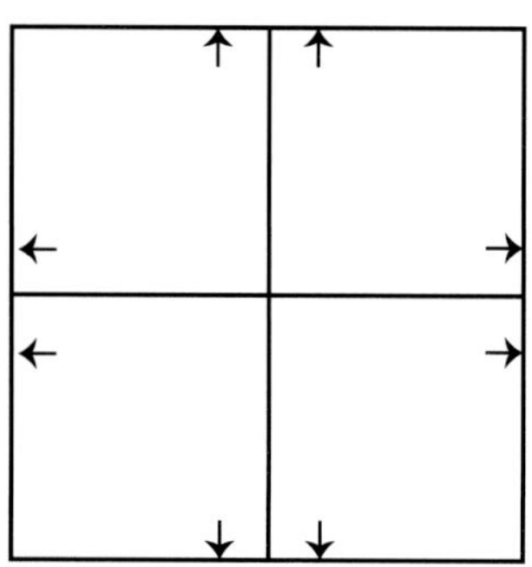

Figure 5–10. Make a placement guide and mark the arrows.

Determine the size the fabric background blocks should be cut by adding ½" for seam allowances to the size of the center square. If the square is 8" x 8", add ½" and cut the fabric blocks 8½" x 8½".

Mysterious Ovals

If the Mysterious Circles pattern can be drafted using a pizza pan, why not try another shape, such as an oval kitchen platter or a roasting pan lid?

Any sized oval object will work for a Mysterious Ovals pattern, and the quilt block will be approximately half the size of the oval object. Thus, an 11⅝" x 15⅝" oval will make a 5¾" x 7¾" quilt block. This is the size used to describe how to draft the pattern.

Supplies

- An oval with smooth even edges
- A piece of poster board at least 2" larger all around than the oval object you are using.
- Two pieces of paper you can see pencil lines through. The paper size should be at least 2" larger all around than the oval shape you are using. I like a product called Fun-dation paper, by HTC. It is 22" wide and is great to draw on and see through.
- Pencils
- Rulers, a long rectangle and a large square

The Pattern

Trace the oval object on the poster board and cut it out. Use the poster board oval to draft the pattern.

Trace the poster board oval on one piece of the see-through paper (Figure 5-11).

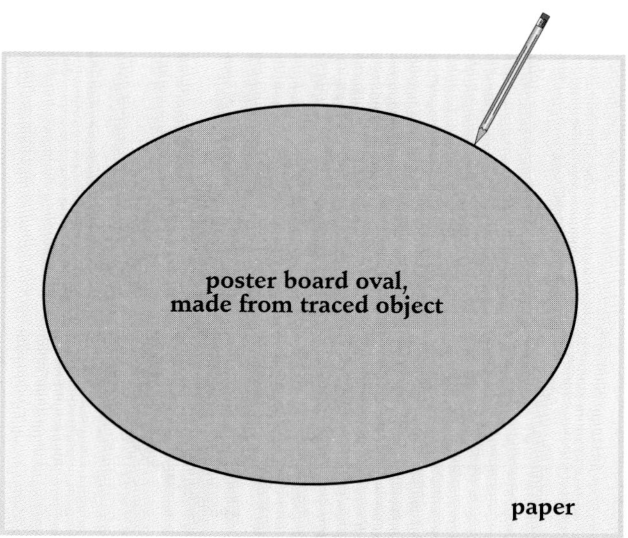

Figure 5–11. Trace the poster board oval.

Fold the paper in half lengthwise, align the traced lines, and finger press a crease (Figure 5–12).

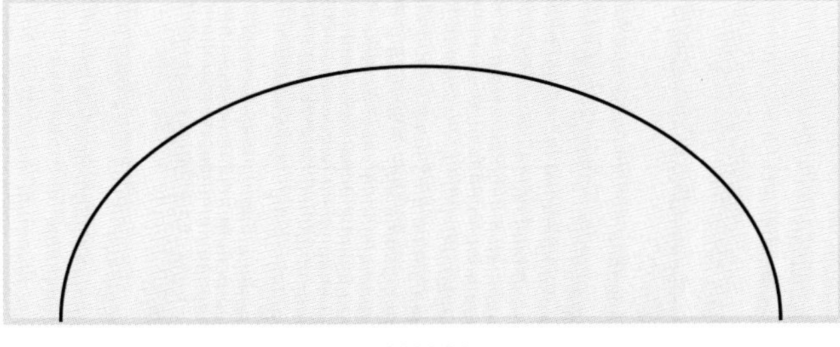

Figure 5–12. Fold the tracing paper in half and crease it.

Unfold the paper, and draw a line along the crease the length of the oval, from end to end. Measure the line, and make a note of this measurement. This is the oval's length (Figure 5–13).

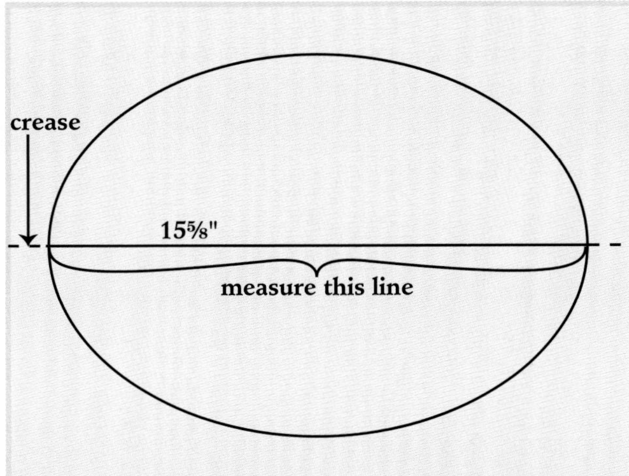

Figure 5–13. Draw a line on the crease, measure the line.

Fold the paper in half in the other direction. Align the traced lines, and finger press a crease (Figure 5–14).

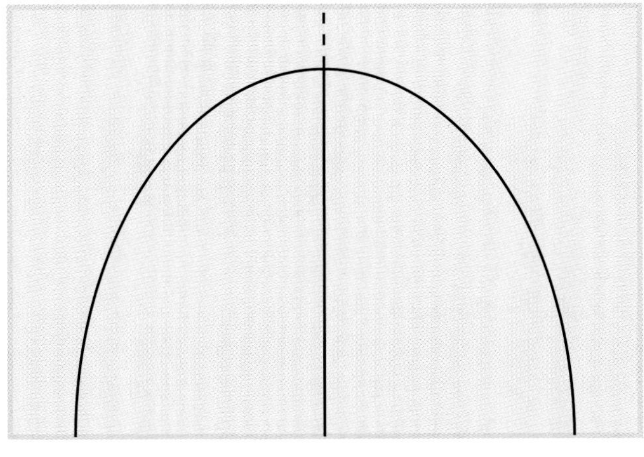

Figure 5–14. Fold the paper in half in the other direction and crease it.

Unfold the paper, and draw a line on the crease along the width of the oval, from side to side. Measure the line, and make a note of this measurement. This is the oval's width (Figure 5–15).

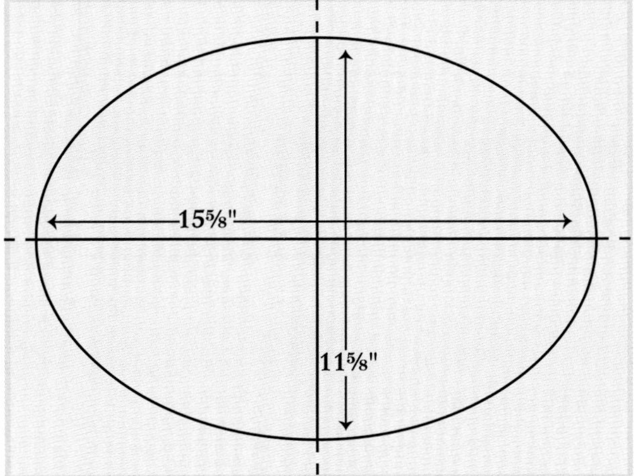

Figure 5–15. Draw a line on the crease and measure it.

Lay the oval poster board pattern on the paper and transfer the lines to the poster board. Set the paper aside (Figure 5–16).

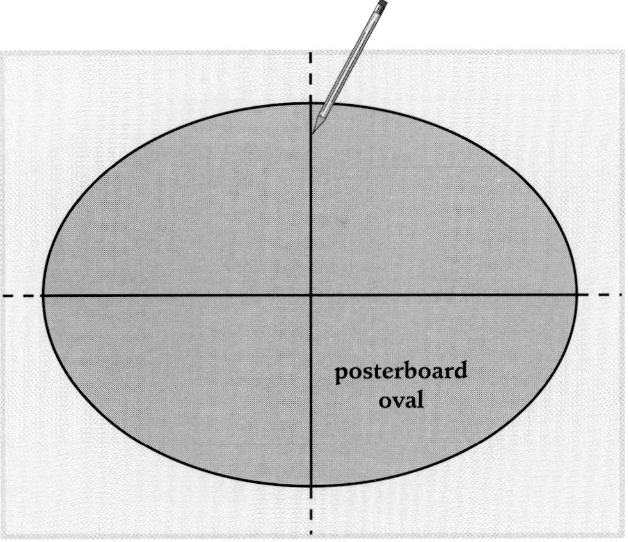

Figure 5–16. Copy the lines on the paper onto the poster board oval.

On the other piece of paper, draw a rectangle the exact size of the oval's measurements. Divide the rectangle into four equal sections. To do this, fold the paper in half, align the pencil lines, and finger press a crease. Open up the paper, and draw a line on the crease. Repeat the process, folding the paper in the other direction (Figure 5–17).

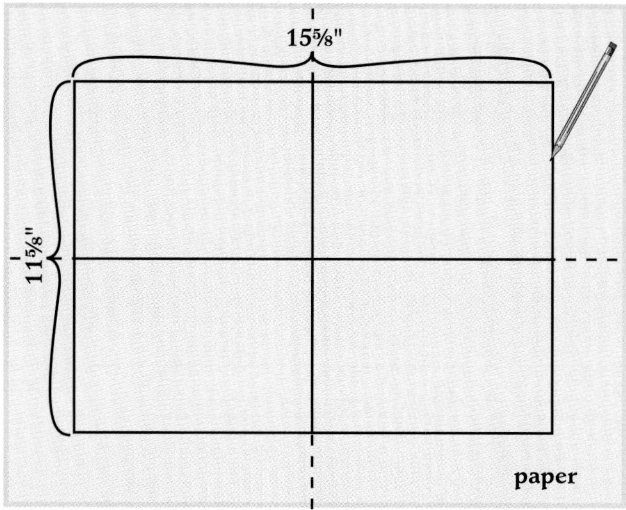

Figure 5–17. Fold the paper rectangle in quarters and draw lines along the folds.

Align the poster board oval lengthwise with the center intersection of the drawn rectangle ,and trace around the poster board oval from corner to corner. Be sure to draw over the center intersecting lines. Repeat on the other side of the traced rectangle (Figure 5–18).

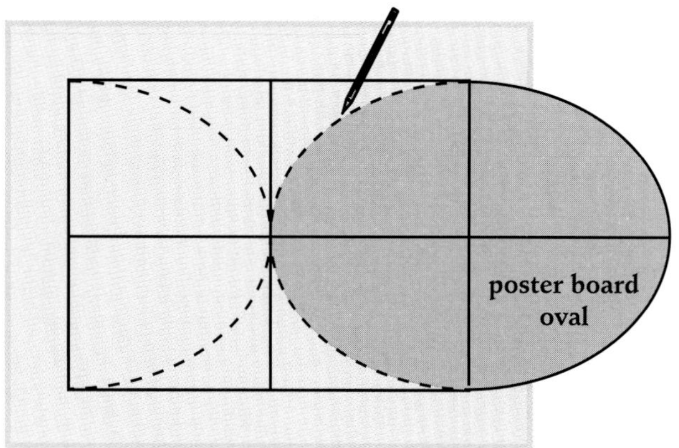

Figure 5–18. Position the poster board oval, and trace around it on both long sides of the rectangle.

Position the poster board oval on one short end of the traced rectangle, aligning the poster board oval with the center intersection of the traced lines. Trace around the oval from corner to corner. Be sure to draw over the center intersecting lines. Repeat on the other end of the traced rectangle (Figure 5–19).

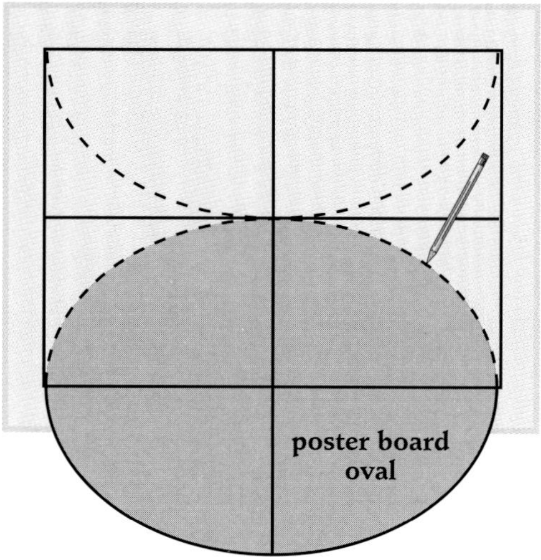

Figure 5–19. Position the poster board oval and trace around it on both ends of the rectangle.

Align the pencil lines on the poster board oval with an outer corner of the rectangle and trace around the poster board oval. Do all four corners (Figure 5–20).

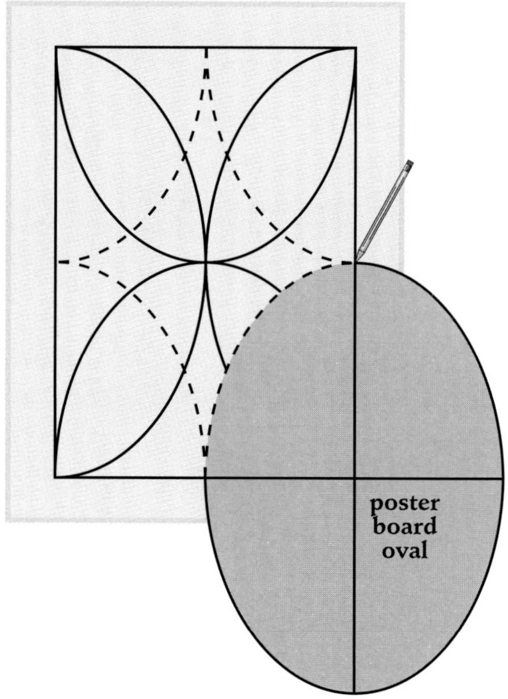

Figure 5–20. Position the poster board oval and trace around it for all corners.

Using a square ruler, isolate the shape in the middle and draw a rectangle around the shape. Be sure all tips are equally squared up. Measure the size of the rectangle and write this size on the paper. With a pencil, draw an arrow at each tip of the shape (Figure 5–21).

Figure 5–21. Draw a rectangle around the central shape, and mark the shape tips with arrows. Measure the size of the rectangle.

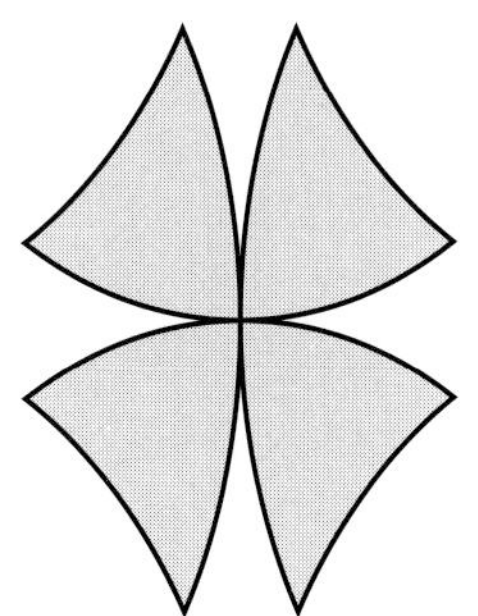

Make a template of the center shape (Figure 5–22).

Figure 5–22. Use the center shape to make a template.

The placement guide is the size of the center rectangle. Transfer the arrows to the guide (Figure 5–23).

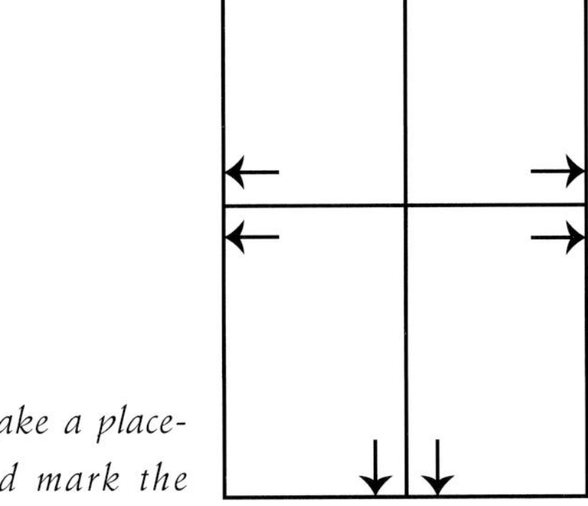

Figure 5–23. Make a placement guide and mark the arrows.

Determine the size the fabric background blocks should be cut by adding ½" to the size of the center rectangle. For example, if the rectangle is 5¾" x 7¾", add ½" and cut the fabric blocks 6¼" x 8¼".

Spinning Circles

This quilt pattern is based on an equilateral triangle. The shape can be any size desired. A shape with a finished size of 3" will be used to describe how to draft the pattern.

Supplies

- Paper, plain or graph
- Ruler with a 60° line
- Pencils
- Compass

The Pattern

Determine the size you want the finished length of the shape to be. The example is 3".

Draw a 3" vertical line and mark the center. Draw a horizontal line that intersects the center of the vertical line (Figure 5–24).

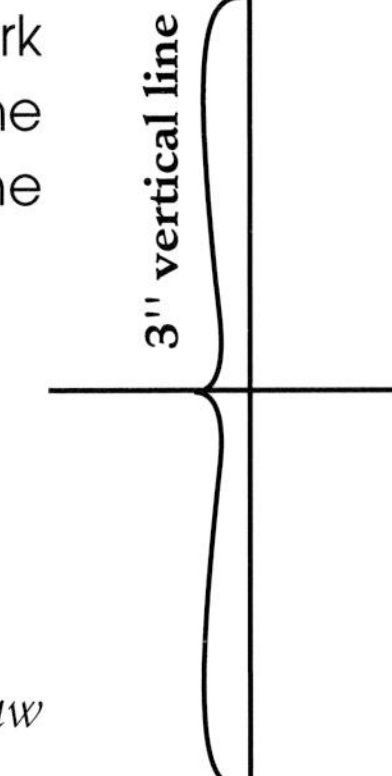

Figure 5–24. Draw a vertical line. Draw a horizontal line through the center.

Place the ruler's 60° line on the 3" vertical line with the edge of the ruler at one end of the 3" line. Draw a 60° line (Figure 5–25).

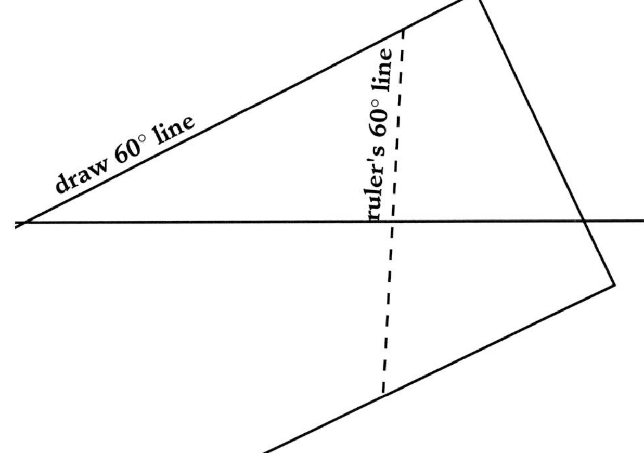

Figure 5–25. Draw a 60° line.

Reposition the ruler and align it with the vertical line to draw lines on the other three sides (Figure 5–26).

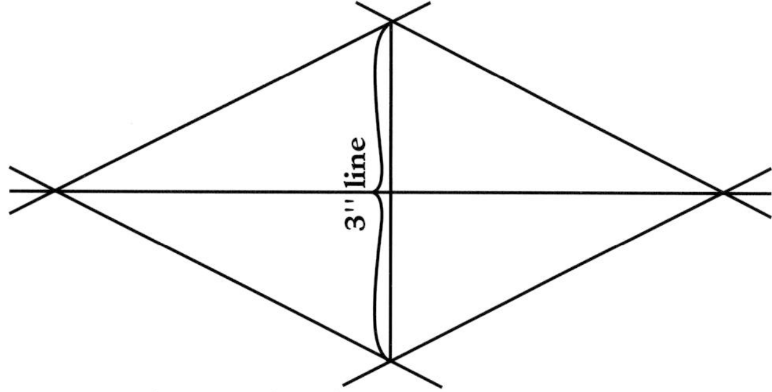

Figure 5–26. Move the ruler and draw the remaining lines.

Starting with the compass point on the tip of the triangle on the horizontal line and the compass pencil on the end of the 3" vertical line, draw half of the shape. Repeat for the opposite side. Make the template from this shape.

To find the distance between the placement lines that will be drawn on the background fabric, measure from the center of the shape to the tip of the triangle on the horizontal line. It's 2⅝" in the example (Figure 5–27).

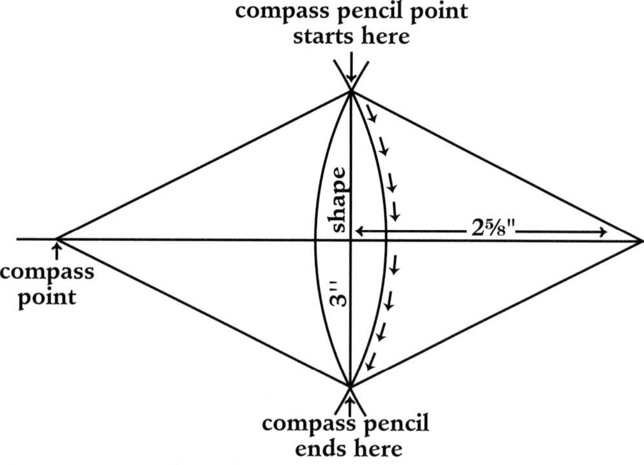

Figure 5–27. Place the compass point on the tip of the triangle on the horizontal line and the pencil on the end of the vertical line. Draw the shape.

On the background fabric, draw the vertical placement lines and the connecting placement lines 2⅝" apart (Figure 5–28).

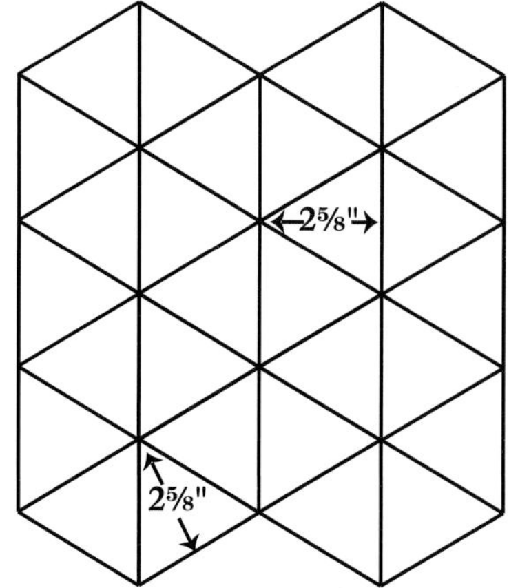

Figure 5–28. Draw placement lines.

Simply Circles

Simply Circles is the easiest pattern to draft. A shape with a finished size of 2" will be used to describe how to draft the pattern.

Supplies

- Paper, plain or graph
- Pencils
- Ruler
- Compass

The Pattern

Determine the size you want the finished length of the shape. The example is 2".

Draw two connected 2" x 2" squares on the paper. Mark the exact center of each square (Figure 5–29).

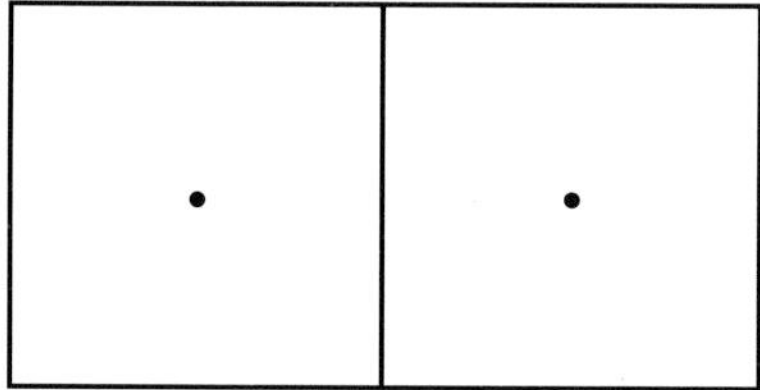

Figure 5–29.

With the compass point on the center of one square and the compass pencil on an end of the connecting line, draw half of the 2" shape. Do the same for the opposite side of the shape (Figure 5–30).

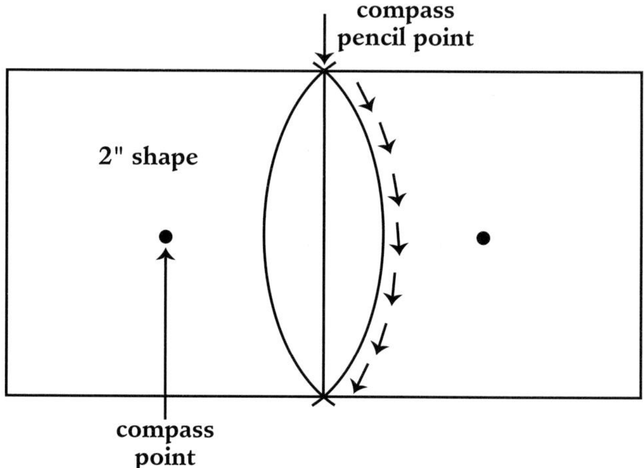

Figure 5–30. Place the compass point on the center of one square and the pencil on one end of the connecting line. Draw one half of the shape. Repeat for the other half. Make the template.

Draw the connecting lines for the shapes 2" apart on the background fabric.

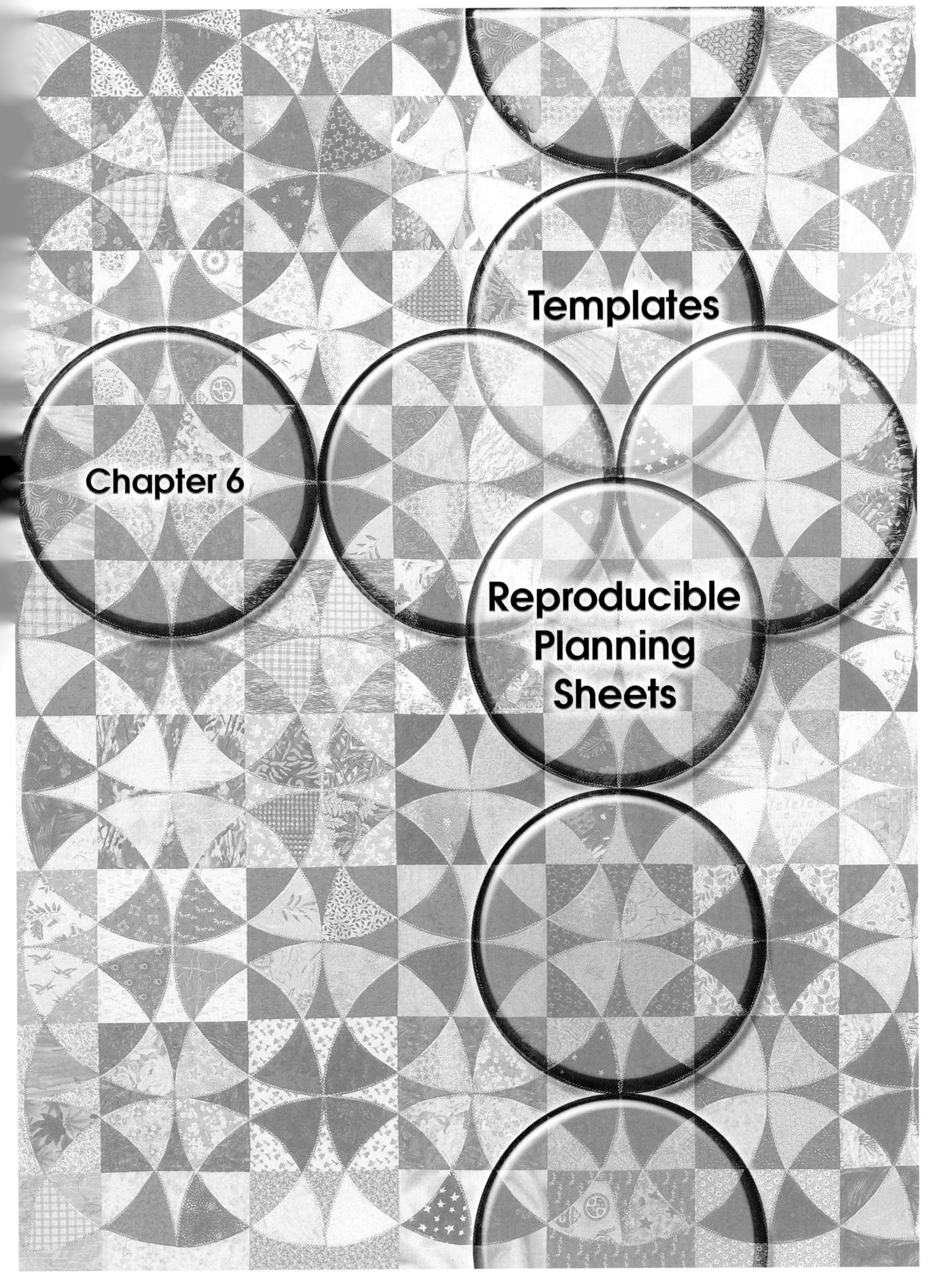

Chapter 6

Templates

Reproducible Planning Sheets

TEMPLATES

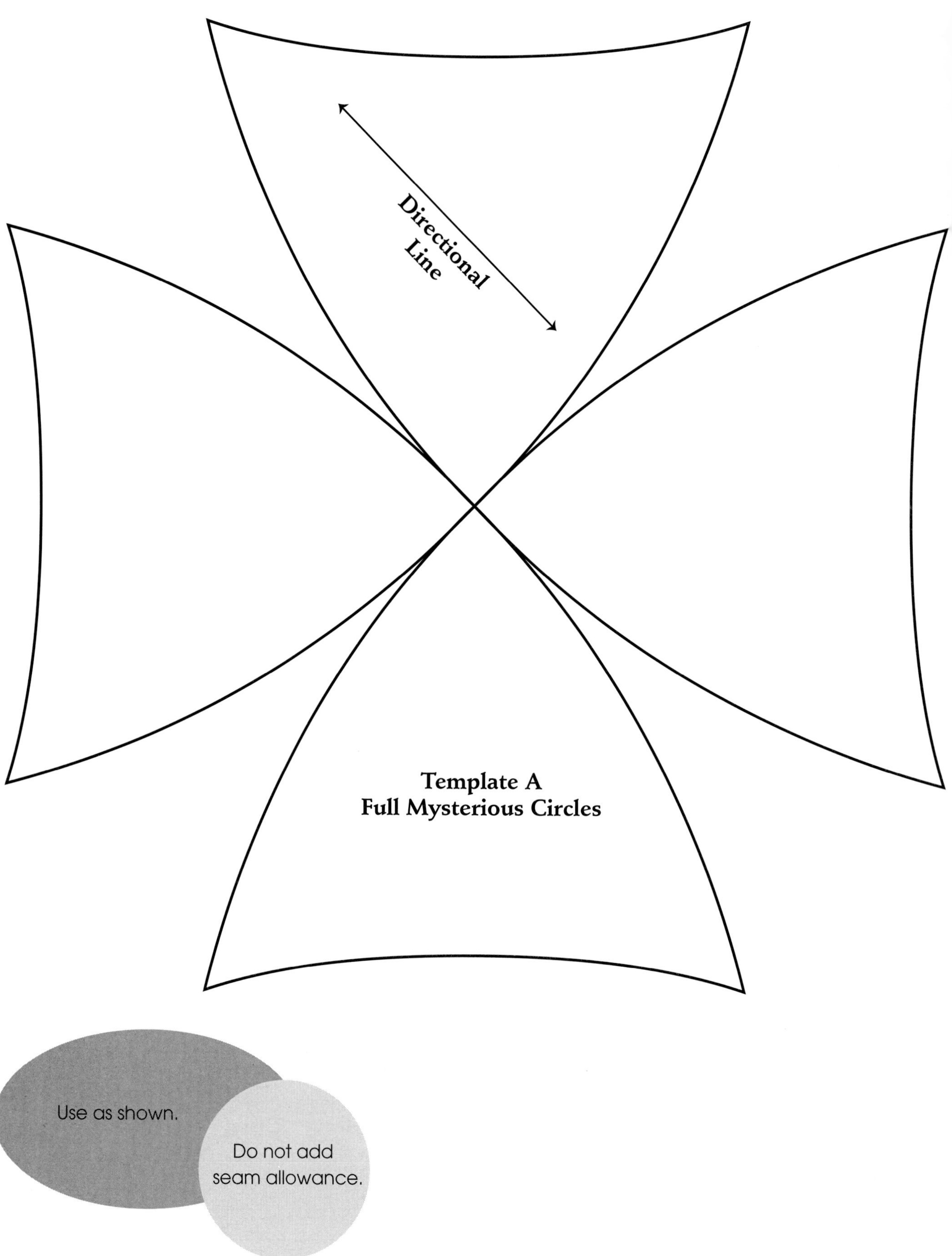

Use as shown.

Do not add seam allowance.

TEMPLATES

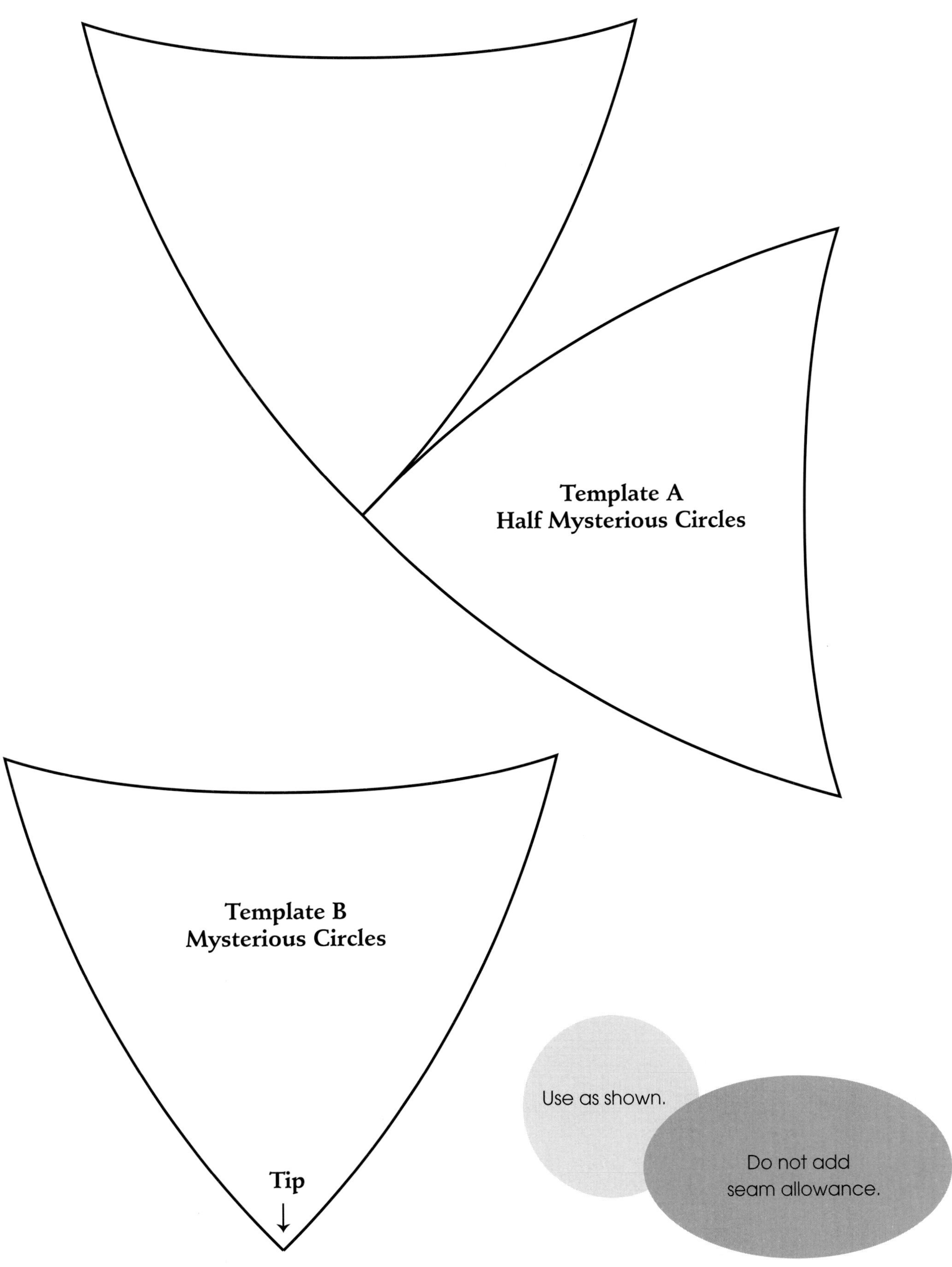
Template A
Half Mysterious Circles
Template B
Mysterious Circles
Tip
Use as shown.
Do not add seam allowance.

TEMPLATES

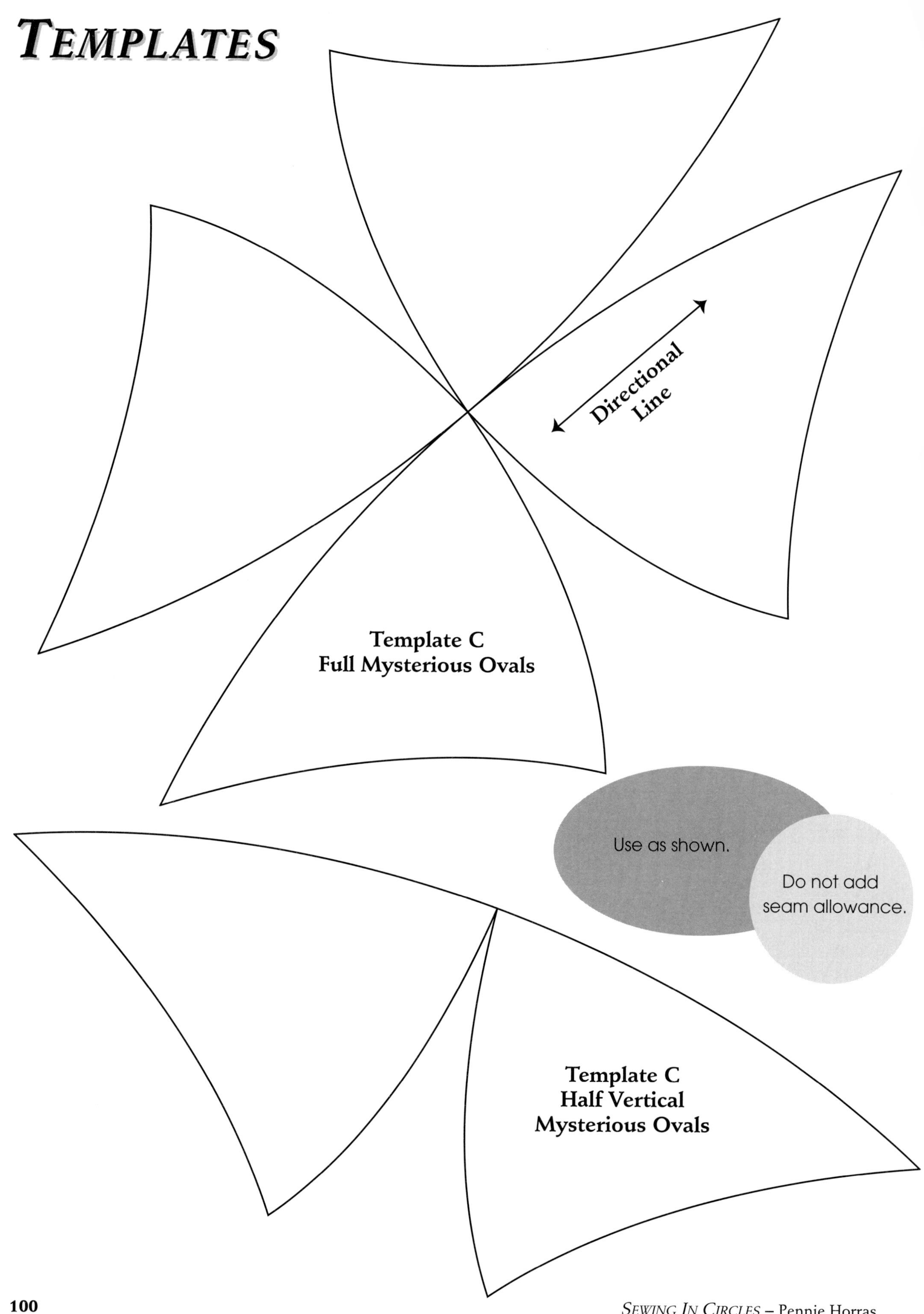
Directional Line
Template C
Full Mysterious Ovals
Use as shown.
Do not add seam allowance.
Template C
Half Vertical
Mysterious Ovals

TEMPLATES

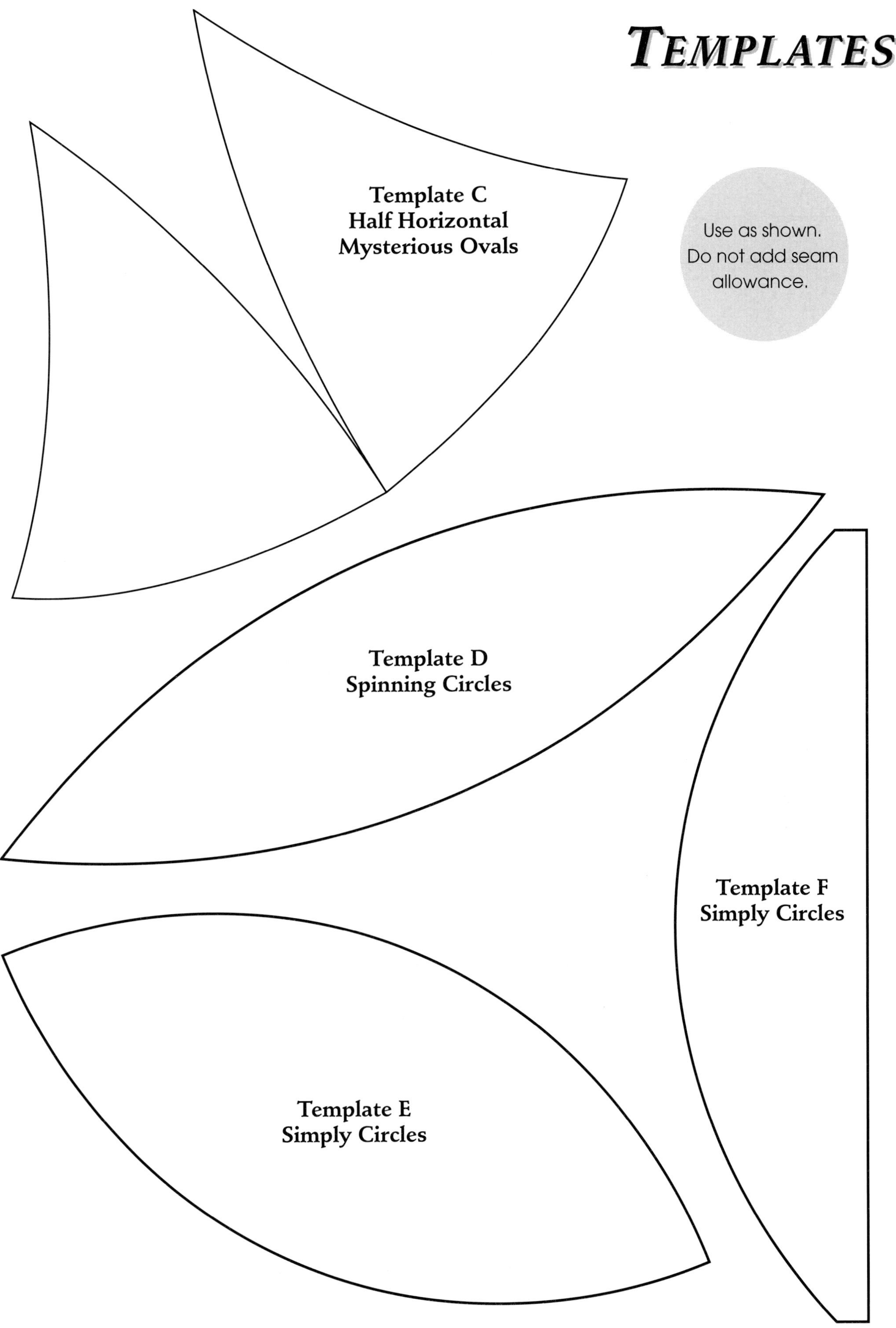
Template C
Half Horizontal
Mysterious Ovals
Use as shown.
Do not add seam
allowance.
Template D
Spinning Circles
Template F
Simply Circles
Template E
Simply Circles

Reproducible Planning Sheets

Use the reproducible planning sheets to help you select color arrangements for a quilt, experiment with new ideas, or just play around and be creative.

Reproducible Planning Sheets

Use the reproducible planning sheets to help you select color arrangements for a quilt, experiment with new ideas, or just play around and be creative.

Reproducible Planning Sheets

Use the reproducible planning sheets to help you select color arrangements for a quilt, experiment with new ideas, or just play around and be creative.

Reproducible Planning Sheets

Use the reproducible planning sheets to help you select color arrangements for a quilt, experiment with new ideas, or just play around and be creative.

Reproducible Planning Sheets

Use the reproducible planning sheets to help you select color arrangements for a quilt, experiment with new ideas, or just play around and be creative.

Reproducible Planning Sheets

Use the reproducible planning sheets to help you select color arrangements for a quilt, experiment with new ideas, or just play around and be creative.

Reproducible Planning Sheets

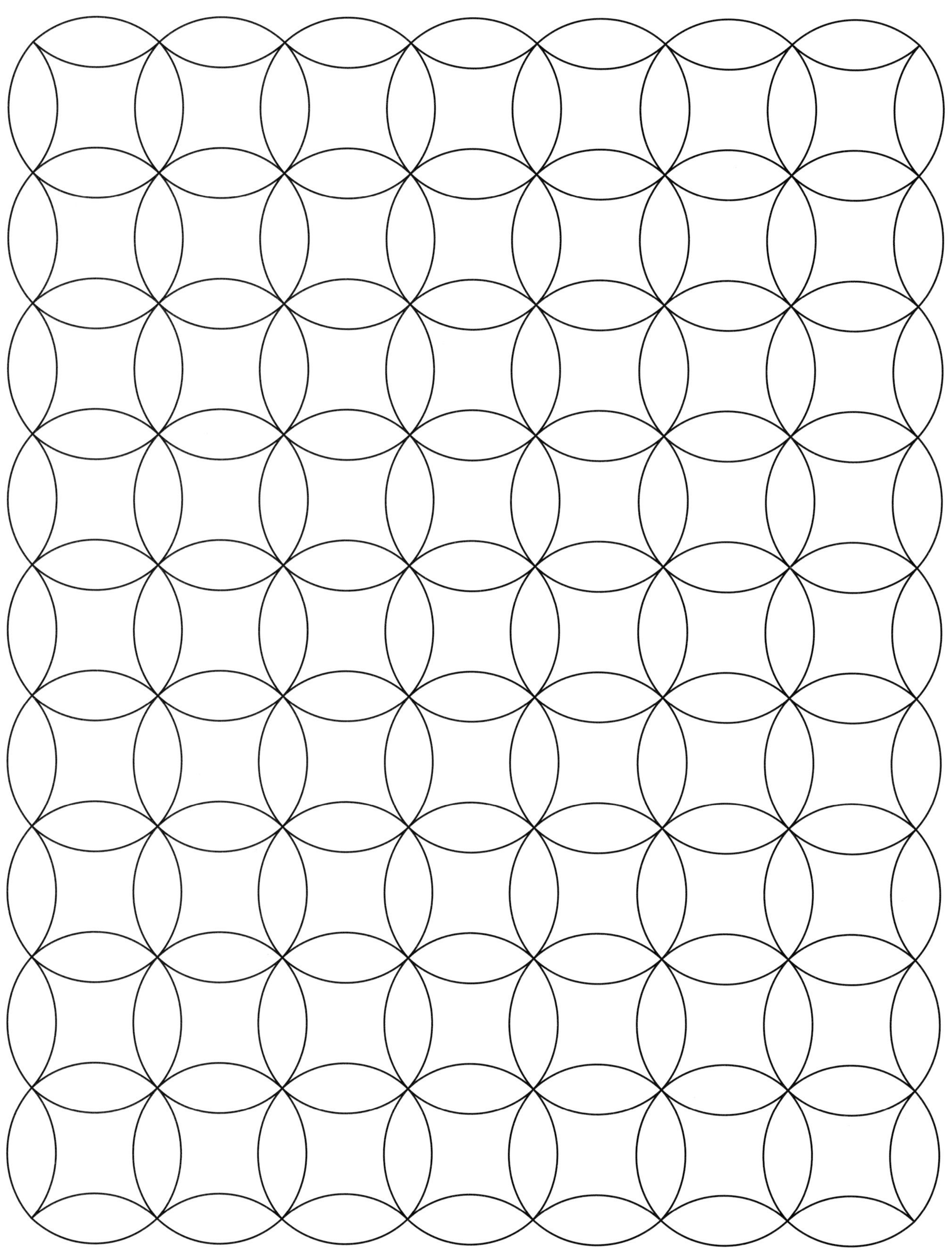

Use the reproducible planning sheets to help you select color arrangements for a quilt, experiment with new ideas, or just play around and be creative.

Reproducible Planning Sheets

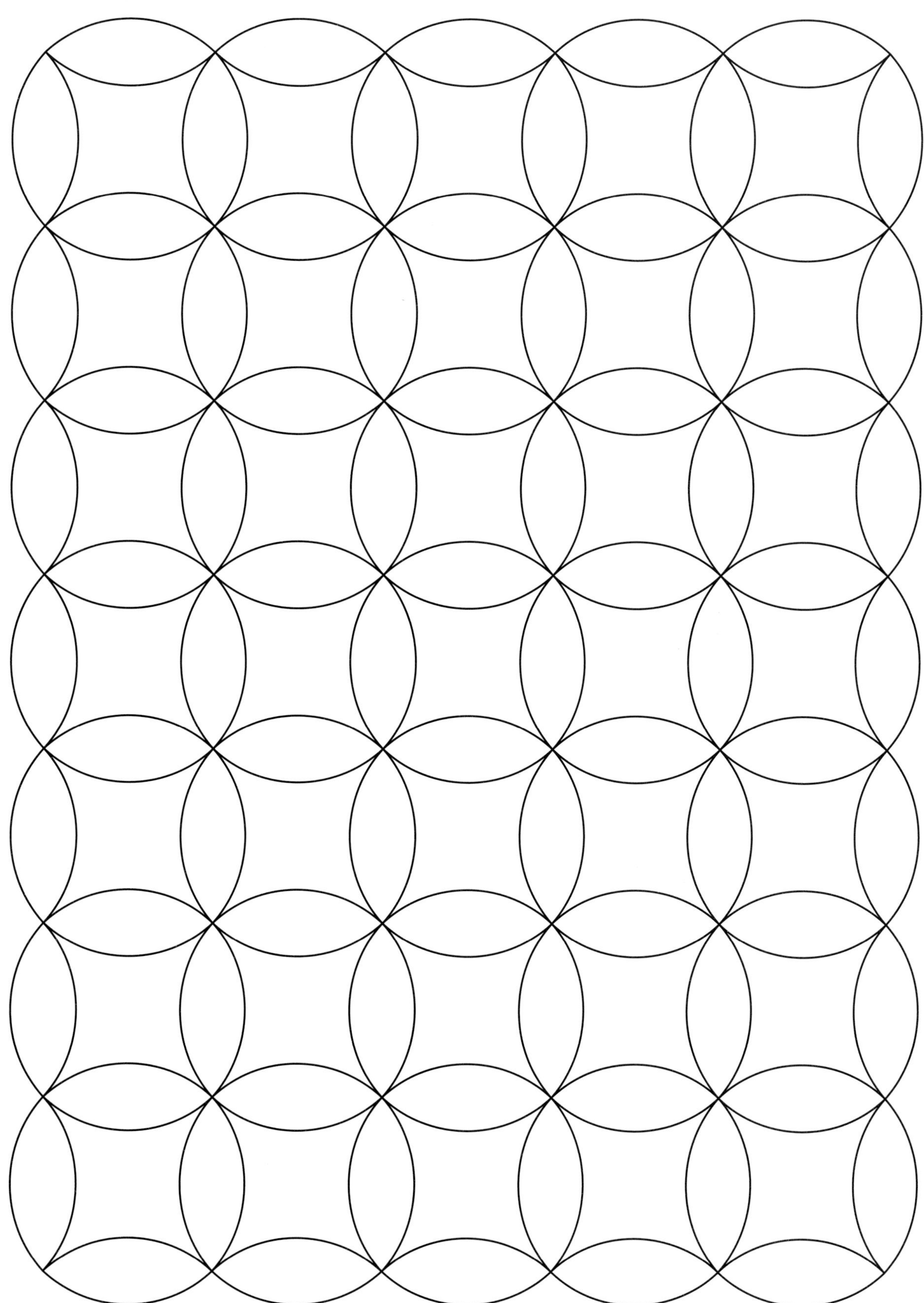

Use the reproducible planning sheets to help you select color arrangements for a quilt, experiment with new ideas, or just play around and be creative.

Bibliography

Brackman, Barbara, *Encyclopedia of Pieced Quilt Patterns.* American Quilter's Society, Paducah, Kentucky, 1993.

Lane, Rose Wilder, *Woman's Day Book of American Needlework.* Simon and Schuster, 1963.

Resources

Hancock's of Paducah
3841 Hinkleville Road
Paducah, KY 42001
1-800-845-8723

Fun-dation paper by HTC

Stitches Galore
109 First Street
Highway 1
Kalona, IA 52247
1-800-233-4189

Fun-dation paper by HTC and Stitch and Ditch by Thread Pro™

About the Author

A Kalona, Iowa, quilt show in the early 1980s was the catalyst that inspired me to try my hand at quiltmaking. I sewed along for years, teaching myself from quilt books, magazines, TV, and trial and error.

The real kickers came when I received an Iowa State Fair blue ribbon for a quilt named HERE COME THE CLOWNS and a viewers' choice award at the International Quilt Festival in Houston, Texas, for YOU'VE COME A LONG WAY, SISTER. These surprising awards so inspired me that I've never looked back. Every quilt I make is documented, and today the count is over 400.

I am very honored to have HERE COME THE CLOWNS included in the *American Quilter's Society 2002 Quilt Art Engagement Calendar* and WE'VE COME A LONG WAY, LADIES accepted in the 2001 AQS quilt show in Paducah, Kentucky. It gave me great pleasure to contribute BETSY'S FLAG to the AQS United We Quilt project, a traveling exhibit of quilts by AQS authors, created in response to the events of September 11, 2001.

My teaching headquarters is Stitches Galore, Kalona, Iowa, and I'm a member of the Northside Strippers quilt guild in Fairfield, Iowa. My life as a quiltmaker is best described in a school paper written by my granddaughter when she was eleven.

Grandma Pennie
by Sarah Johnston

My Grandma Pennie is a relative that interests me with her beautiful quilts.

Grandma wears jeans and t-shirts. She wears cheap tennis shoes from WalMart that get holes in them because she walks so much. Grandma has a fun personality and laughs all the time. Grandma Pennie knows a lot about making quilts but is always learning more.

Grandma lives in an awesome house in the country with her husband and one of her sons on a farm. Each morning, after everybody has left and the house is quiet, Grandma goes to her sewing room. She usually gets tired after a while so she takes a nap, but she goes back to work later on.

"Where do you get your ideas for your quilts?" I asked Grandma once. "Well," she said with a laugh, " I think that the spirit of an old quilter has taken over my body and is using me to create the quilts that she didn't have time to make." She then added, "I think that quiltmaking is just in my genes and my ideas are just naturally there."

Grandma, like an artist, is very creative and is good with her hands. I have learned that my grandma is very patient with her work and takes time to make it beautiful. She loves to make quilts and has taught me a few things about making them. I have found that it is hard work and you must have a knack for it.

Other AQS Books

This is only a small selection of the books available from the American Quilter's Society. AQS books are known worldwide for timely topics, clear writing, beautiful color photos, and accurate illustrations and patterns. The following books are available from your local bookseller, quilt shop, or public library.

#6076 us$21.95

#6210 us$24.95

#6074 us$21.95

#5755 us$21.95

#6212 us$25.95

#6000 us$24.95

#6207 us$16.95

#5848 us$19.95

#6078 us$19.95